I

FAMILY MEETING HANDBOOK

Here for Each Other, Hearing Each Other

by Katherine Foldes

Printed in the United States of America

First printing 2015

ISBN 978-0-9966847-0-5
Parenting. Children. Family. Communication.

Katherine Foldes
kathyfoldes@gmail.com

Cover Design and graphics by Blossom Liu

DEDICATION

This book is dedicated to my precious family—and to yours.

ACKNOWLEDGEMENTS

I would like to acknowledge everyone who helped and encouraged me throughout the long process of bringing this book into being. I thank my husband and children who contributed so much to the content and writing of this book and who encouraged me often to complete the book. I thank those of you who read and edited early and late versions—John Hunt, Tom Hunt, Carolyn Hunt, Debby Guyol, Janis Adler, Debra Meadow, Marcy Sacks, and Jessie Sandrock. Special thanks to my daughter for her helpful suggestions, initial graphics and her formatting help. To my writing group Giselle Bawnik and Anne Castleton and to Karen Braucher Tobin. To my workshop participants who brought me much joy and many stories they allowed me to use. To my colleagues at Oregon Women Lawyers who gave me the opportunity to present the premise for this book. And to all of you out there who will benefit from Family Meetings.

"The kids are very keen to have their own issues addressed, particularly the seven year old." LN

TABLE OF CONTENTS SUMMARY

Detailed Table of contents

Now what do we say to our children about them?

How can we make the meetings "good" for our family? What You Already Know About Good Meetings and Tips

What are the ten steps involved in holding a successful Family Meetings? Overview

Now the Specifics:

The Seven Elements that ensure that your meetings build your family

What do you do if one person talks too much or another one doesn't want to talk at all? How do you share the time?

Ground Rules and Related Questions. How can we create that safe space for conversations?

Why at least one positive item in each meeting?

Why write decisions down—it seems so formal?

Why are regular Family Meetings so important?

Preface

Family Meetings changed my life. I hope they will change yours. I wrote this handbook to share what I discovered "by accident"—a process for creating the kind of family life most of us long for. More than twenty five years ago, my husband and I were trying yet another way to deal with a child who would not sleep through the night. We tried a Family Meeting with our two and a half year old son. Our Family Meeting did not solve this problem, yet it was an amazingly positive experience. Our son, at two and a half, came up with some suggestions on how he could sleep through the night! From then on, we continued holding Family Meetings; through them we experienced closeness and communication with our son and later with our daughter and, of course, with one another.

When all of the things that happen in families happened in ours, we brought them to our Family Meetings-- upsetting things like the death of a grandparent or situations at school or work. Sometimes they were things we, the parents, felt strongly about such as the amount of time spent in front of electronic devices, and sometimes the meetings were about staying in tune with the natural changes over time such as bedtime, teen driving and more. We always had at least one fun item in our Family Meetings; we planned birthday parties and family vacations, all of which were successful since everyone had contributed their ideas.

Setting aside this regular time made an enormous difference in our family life. It emphasized the importance of family and affirmed each member's uniqueness as an individual. We really know one another in our family; we remain close to our young adult children and they to one another. When our son turned eighteen, he told us, "Mom and Dad, even though I never liked Family Meetings, I'm glad you had them. I'm sure I would have been a rebellious teenager without them." Both of our children have said that they intend to hold Family Meetings when they have children. Why? Because they are a simple way to give the most important messages we all need—YOU COUNT AND YOU BELONG! Through Family Meetings, we created a safe space, the safe haven we all want our home to be.

I began to share what I had learned about building a great family life by creating a Family Meetings Workshop twelve years ago. The feedback from parents who attended the workshops has been amazing. We held "reunions" for workshop participants as a way of encouraging parents to continue with Family Meetings over time and to share their stories with other families. Many have continued to hold Family Meetings to this day, finding them a valuable part of their parenting. Others have stopped and then resumed after a problem arose. The workshop participants and parents I've mentioned the book to-- even those who don't normally read parenting books-- have encouraged me to write about Family Meetings. I've also been asked by pastors and counselors to share what I have learned. This book is for all of you.

"The kids (ages 7, 5 and 2 ½), are all excited when we have a Family Meeting planned. We have told our good friends and neighbors about Family Meetings, specifically that we feel they are a powerful way to be more connected as a family, to show that everyone's opinions and ideas are important, and as a way to try to improve communication. It has helped the kids start to see that family is a safe, important place to let your feelings, concerns, fears and ideas be heard. It has been a very good forum for us parents to feel like we can talk to the kids about unwanted or unacceptable behaviors and have them help problem-solve better behaviors in a calm and more rational atmosphere than in the heat of some frustrating moment. I noticed a deeper sense of connection to my husband and to the kids, and the kids are learning that it is important to express feelings to others and to try and communicate well." VM

Introduction

Want a great home life? Most people do. Family Meetings can get you there. With Family Meetings, you can more intentionally build a family that reflects your hopes and dreams as parents. What do I mean by "intentionally"? Most parents give thought to the basic physical needs of their children, especially in their early years—safety, food, sleep, warmth, those sorts of issues. Many parents believe that the rest of family life takes care of itself; as parents, they will react to situations as they come up. But think about this--what would happen if we purposefully think and plan for a great family life—about how we can create cooperation, respect, connection, familiarity, love, responsibility, communication, closeness and comfort. Many books have been written about the content of these concepts; this book is about the process to gain all of these wonderful qualities.

So why not apply the same thoughtfulness we give to creating a happy, healthy family as we do about what to feed the baby? Why not take the time? Think about it. Reacting as situations arise is a piece-meal approach to parenting. Parents often react in the moment, rather than respond thoughtfully and in advance. Parents often have a hard time keeping up with each age and stage of their children's lives and so aren't able to make a good decision at the time a decision is needed. Family life then wears down parental resolve or affection or worse yet, may create a world of unintended consequences in the children.

This book is for you if you have ever

- Wondered how to stay somewhere between permissive and domineering in your (or your partner's) parenting.
- Puzzled about whether you are over or under-involved in your child's life.
- Expressed frustration with making decisions on the spot in response to "Can I, why can't I" requests.
- Heard yourself sound like your own mother or father in the way you vowed you never would.

- Longed for cooperation from your family members.
- Felt like you are always the "bad guy" or the nag.
- Wanted to know what's going on in your child's life.
- Felt too rushed to parent the way you know you "should."

This book will answer your questions:

1. **Why should we and how do we hold Family Meetings?**
2. **How do I introduce the idea of Family Meetings to my family?**
3. **How do we, as a busy family, make time for Family Meetings?**
4. **How early in our children's lives should we start having Family Meetings?**
5. **How often should we hold them?**
6. **How can we remain in our parenting role if we give children a say?**
7. **Are Family Meetings for us if there is only one parent or only one child?**

This is a handbook with exercises that will guide you through the thought process and help you create a wonderful family life. Take a moment to do the exercises, share them with your parenting partner(s) and you will see the benefit. Read the question and answer sections to learn the practical steps of Family Meetings and many real examples of how Family Meetings benefit real families.

For example, do you know any families like the following?

Family 1: Leslie and Hank had high expectations of their children, i.e. to do better in every arena than they themselves had done. Leslie and Hank came from big families with limited means and limited parental attention. They wanted only the best for their children; partly because they had not had the opportunities, they tried to provide them for their children. Leslie became a stay-at-home mom and devoted herself to shepherding the children through many extracurricular activities, starting when the children were preschoolers. Hank coached the sports of the two boys as soon as they could play sports. Sometimes the parents were exhausted by the schedules they kept with their children. The boys had every new computer program or device and were proficient in their use. They achieved excellence in every activity from sports to academics to special competitions in math, debate and Honor Society. The two boys went to the best colleges. Once there, things began to fall apart. One son developed an eating disorder and the other cocooned in his room until the Dean of Students called his parents.

Family 2: Kelly and Maria didn't want to repeat the mistakes of their parents. Kelly's parents had overly high expectations of her and Maria's parents left her to raise herself while they worked full-time and devoted attention to her demanding older sister. As parents themselves, Kelly and Maria befriended their children but did not intrude. Their older daughter spent increasing amounts of time with friends from an early age, did poorly in school, got in trouble with the law occasionally but was very sweet when at home. She lost motivation and is not prepared for college or the work world now that she is a young adult.

Family 3: Tracey and Bob held Family Meetings with their children from the time they were five and eight years old. Tracey was the child of an alcoholic parent in a home where this secret was well-kept. Bob came from a family where parents were kind but not very involved with their children. Both Tracey and Bob wanted better communication and balance in their family life-- and in their parenting-- than they had experienced themselves as children.

Through periodic Family Meetings, their family decided that spending time together was a priority; they set aside time to plan monthly outings and a yearly vacation with activities each family member would enjoy. They negotiated how many extracurricular activities family members could be comfortably involved in (both children and adults). They negotiated about how much time each spent in front of a screen (phone, computer, TV, or video game). In their Family Meetings, they checked in with one another periodically about how friendships were going, how work and school were going and what kind of support or help the family member might want. Their two girls had various problems with relationships and with school but these were caught early and resolved by the children with input and support from Tracey and Bob. By the time the girls were off to college, they were well set for independence, having held summer jobs. They had direction and motivation to succeed and were well-connected with family and friends.

As you can see from these stories, one benefit of Family Meetings is that they keep so many aspects of family life “in the middle.” What do I mean by “in the middle?” I mean a good balance between too much involvement and too little, between permissiveness and authoritarian parenting, between balancing work and family, school and home. But that is that is not the only benefit of Family Meetings. Read on…..

Why Have Family Meetings?

Are you like other parents, wishing that your child came with a manual? Wondering how you can keep up as children continually grow and change? Do you ever wish for a parenting handbook that would tell you exactly how to address every problem with your child in just the right way? While there are many parenting books out there, no manual will ever written for beings as complex as humans.

Regular, meaningful two-way communication is the key to a happy, healthy family; however most parenting books focus on developmental information, on particular challenges, or on troubling aspects of modern life rather than on a holistic approach. Not this one. The Family Meetings Handbook is a pro-active, preventative approach to parenting that goes beyond just getting through life with your children to purposefully creating a wonderful family life.

Family Meetings build on the knowledge that small groups, meeting over a period of time, will improve communication and will create a closer bond between members. We know this in the context of organizations. Team meetings, if done well, increase effectiveness and satisfaction of their members. It is time to bring this wisdom to our family lives. We already know quite a bit about effective meetings from our work, from sports or volunteer experiences. Here, we will learn how to adapt this knowledge to family life.

How do Family Meetings create a great family life? It's simple. Family Meetings give all members three important messages—"You count," "You belong," and "You are safe here." Everyone listens, everyone speaks. Never underestimate the power of being heard. Listening is a technique that is often used in therapy. With Family Meetings, your children may not need therapy. Of course, it's not that simple. Our society makes it likely that at some time in life, everyone will need therapy. The point is that we adults often speak of our own childhoods-- in which we felt unheard or didn't feel we belonged; we hear about being given material things but not feeling loved or cherished. All of these difficulties can be prevented by Family Meetings. By holding Family Meetings over time, with the intent to create a great family, parents get:

- communication with respect-what you give is likely to be what you get when it comes to respect. Family Meetings lead to respectful children who don't need to rebel.
- better behavior- children learn the reasons behind the rules and know that their opinion counts. They are more likely to become invested in the rules.
- updates from each family member- kids become invested in their family life and their own future .

- joint problem solving- kids feel safe talking about issues that come up.
- parenting better as a team—parents can be clear about their styles and beliefs and this clarity leads to better teamwork.
- more positive attention on each member and on family life to counter the natural tendency for love to be worn away over time by the pressures and challenges of daily life.
- a time and place to bring up the hard issues more easily- sexuality, alcohol, drugs, death, the meaning of life and more.
- time to plan what the family wants to do or to become.
- rules or family policies which change over time so that they remain age-appropriate.

Parents often end up following the "easy road" or just the opposite, over-managing their children. We parents are very good at rationalizing.

"All kids do this these days."
"My child is so independent; she can play by herself for hours."
"Computers and TV's are so educational nowadays."
"I'm right here if my child needs me."

When parents operate from either extreme of permissiveness or micro-managing, all too often the results we see in children are negative. Children can end up without the motivation, self-discipline or organizational skills and end up with their future independence compromised. Or just the reverse, children become over-achievers, always looking for outside validation, resulting in eventual burn-out in adult life. This book is all about how to achieve a "happy medium," with the cooperation and involvement of children within constraints established by parents.

"Parenting can feel so all alone and then it's hard when there's a power struggle and I feel dumb in taking the bait." Workshop participant

Conveying love-we love our children and we all want our children to feel loved, but how do we accomplish this? Some parents wind up with over-indulged or over-scheduled children. Showing love effectively consists of

- *listening to your child*
- *having a forum for telling a child that he or she is loved or appreciated*
- *creating an environment where the child has a say without whining,*
- *the child learns what the parents' values are directly from them*

A pitch for purposeful parenting. In every other important area of our life, we think about and make plans, but in our parenting we often just don't want to do it. Some of my Family Meetings workshop participants have raised the argument that their home life is the one place where they cherish spontaneity rather than intentionality.

There are advantages to spontaneity in parenting, fun being among the first of these. When we are open and have few expectations, there is the possibility of doing or saying what otherwise might not be done or said. Some examples are deciding to go to the park on the spur of the moment, joking, roughhousing, or blowing bubbles in the yard. These spontaneous moments are precious. They are the essence of family time. "See what unfolds" is the motto of spontaneity. Certainly spontaneity in family life and in parenting is an essential ingredient to happiness. If we didn't have spontaneity when would we sneak in a hug, a tickle; or when would we chase our child, make up jokes, grant a wish, or seize an opportunity to learn something surprising. Spontaneity is good for bonding, good for spicing up our everyday life. Spontaneity also teaches us how to be flexible; flexibility is important in the increasingly structured environment in which children live. It is particularly refreshing to working parents who have so many deadlines and demands. Oh, to not have any “shoulds” hanging over us, to have time to play. Yes, spontaneity is important.

As with any value taken to the extreme, spontaneity can become a negative. Family Meetings are about restoring balance.

Without some intentionality, when do we actually step back and take a look at how our family is evolving, how our values are being lived both as adults, as parents and as children? Without intentionality, the activity of the moment, the whining of the moment or “The Schedule”, often takes over the concerns of people. When is it a good time to have that talk about sexuality, about death, about what’s important in life, about what the good life really is?

Family Meetings provide a simple structure to convey priorities and to bring family members into a closer relationship that lasts a lifetime. An hour a month, or even once a quarter, can make this difference. Family Meetings may actually add to your family's fun when you use Family Meetings to set the date for outings and vacations.

The work analogy: have you ever met a bad boss who is non-responsive so you don't know where you stand? You feel low in priority while having to struggle to figure it out on your own. Or have you experienced a boss who either lacks planning or imposes plans without consulting the people who actually execute them? Have you met the boss who doesn't take the time to develop policies to guide the employees he or she supervises and ends up spending more time deciding each issue on a case by case basis? Or a boss who imposes plans from above? How was that for you, the person who actually did the work? A bad boss influences the whole atmosphere and satisfaction in the workplace.

By contrast, consider the boss who takes into account the needs of others, asks what these needs are and can articulate the responses of others. People under such a boss feel important and included in the process of moving

forward as a team. Good leaders likewise acknowledge others; they work with others toward agreed upon goals. But better yet, good leaders plan ahead and their intentionality influence the workplace for the good. These same leadership qualities actually apply to parents in a family. Parents are the leaders, the role models, the supervisors and the creators of the family unit. These are just a few examples of the importance of addressing respect and teamwork in the family with intentionality. The family is where we live the most meaningful part of our lives—or it could be.

Yes, It's Worth the Effort.

How do I know that Family Meetings work? From my own twenty years of experience and from the workshops on Family Meetings. I have checked back with participants over time and included many of their amazing, positive stories in each chapter.

"My kids light up at the prospect of having a meeting where they have their say and have

continued to love Family Meetings. My kids remind me of when the meeting is scheduled!"

"Through the Family Meeting even the mundane subject of chores can bring the whole family closer and convey the messages- "we all count" and "we all belong" through dealing with "we all contribute" to the family."

What's in this book? Answers to Your Questions!

This book outlines the steps of Family Meetings and tips on how to hold great Family Meetings. Exercises guide you. The steps are clear and they are straightforward.

Good meeting process is not enough by itself to ensure the kind of communication and bonding that create a wonderful family life. We need also to pay attention to the quality or "spirit" of these meetings. This book contains a step by step "how to" section on Family Meetings and answers your "nuts and bolts" questions.

Next, communication skills and tips help you build the quality of your interactions with your children. Creating a safe space for family discussion is the key to creating a wonderful family life.

<u>Chapter One:</u> answers frequently asked questions, ones that you may be asking right now. Family Meetings most likely will be something new. How do I get started? What's the best age to start them? What are the steps? These and many more of your questions are answered in this section. Look for tips and examples to help your Family Meetings succeed.

<u>Chapter Two</u>: parents prepare before they call the first Family Meeting. Please don't be tempted to skip the preparation! Not only reading the exercises, but actually doing them. Why? As with so many other activities, the prep work ensures a good result. Think of painting a wall. Would you

paint without cleaning and sanding and expect the paint job to hold up? No. The prep work in this book provides the foundation for building your family through Family Meetings. The exercises are intended to help you create the family you want, based on the positive messages and beliefs you select to convey to your children. Start from a brief survey of how things are going in your family now, then turn to the exercises about messages and beliefs, hopes, fears and expectations about parenting and family life. Take the time to find out your parenting partner's views. Articulating these to one another in a safe space is a Family Meeting in its own right but it is also the way to really find out how similar or different you are in your values and methods of parenting, how satisfied you and your parenting partner are with your current family life and more. Through this understanding, parents can purposefully go toward their hopes and away from their fears. The last exercise in this section asks what you think Family Meetings will accomplish for you and also for your family as a whole. You will be motivated to start your own family's meetings by doing these four exercises!

Chapter Three: answers frequently asked general questions about Family Meetings such as how old the child or children need to be, how to introduce the idea to your children and much more.

Chapter Four: addresses how to hold the Family Meeting itself, the "nuts and bolts" of Family Meetings. You will recognize several of the steps from meetings you have attended in other settings. This chapter has both an overview and then details and tips on each step. It also includes stories from parents about what they have learned from their Family Meetings. As with most processes involving people, it's not the steps that are hard. What's hard is doing the steps over and over again for an extended period of time—and with an open mind and in a spirit of cooperation. How do we keep Family Meeting's fresh over the changing years of childhood? Look for answers in Chapters Four and beyond.

Chapter Five: briefly summarizes the ages and stages of children's development and then suggests Family Meeting topics for each age group. Use this chapter if you and your children need ideas on what's relevant to each stage of childhood. One purpose in including these topics is to emphasize that Family Meetings are not called primarily to address specific problems. Family Meetings are ongoing. Let's give attention to each family member on how things are going so that we can keep up with our changing children. Family Meetings are a safe place to convey that each person belongs and each is valued.

Chapter Six is a script of a sample Family Meeting. Feel free to use this as a model for your own first Family Meeting. It's only a sample; be creative and inventive and you will have Family Meetings that are tailored to your family.

Chapter Seven: Family Meetings over the long haul addresses obstacles and solutions. How can you and your family sustain the effort of holding Family Meetings over time? Workshop participants share their ideas on overcoming the common obstacles—lack of time, scheduling conflicts, the pull of work and many others. Yes, it's tempting to resist the idea of holding these meetings for an indefinite period of time. Instead of becoming parents who whine about the commitment, why not be pro-active and use the ideas in this chapter to overcome your resistance and the natural obstacles that arise.

Chapter Eight: summarizes expert advice on how to communicate effectively. Much of the information in this chapter is often conveyed in therapy or counseling only after there is a problem. Family Meetings are intentional way to prevent problems, so why not look over this list to see if there are ways to improve your own communication with your children and with your fellow parent--and even better, to teach better communication to your growing children.

Chapter Nine: More Stories and Examples. Hear about the actual experiences of parents and children. Some families have held meetings for many years, others for just a few months.

Now on to the "meat" of this book!

CHAPTER ONE: Why Have Family Meetings?

???

The Six Main Benefits of Family Meetings

1. **Taking Stock and Correcting Course**

Family Meetings are great for "course corrections" for parents and children alike. They provide a periodic way to look at parents' behavior--whether parents are too involved with children or too absent, too strict or too permissive. And for children-- are they involved in too many or too few activities, are they making good progress at school or with organizational and life skills. Many parents don't take the time to take stock on a regular basis. Many parents just let things happen but, you aren't one of them. You picked up this book. Even with lots of thought and care in parenting, there are no guarantees of good outcomes, so why not give it your best shot?

Contrast these two stories.

Helen and Jim "discover" that their daughter can't graduate high school because she doesn't have minimum competency in math due to a learning disability. They are infuriated with the school and feel blind-sided. However, all through the years, they had adopted a hands-off attitude and considered their daughter's school difficulties a lack of motivation. "If you just try harder," they told her over and over. It was not a two-way conversation. The daughter's self-esteem was poor, her options few. Eventually she graduated through a GED program and works in a service job.

Laura and Kim thought that periodic Family Meetings with their children were important. After their son experienced difficulty learning to read in second grade, the Family Meeting included taking stock and asking clarifying questions to find out the child's perspective. The child couldn't really articulate the reasons he couldn't read but was able to tell his parents how hard it was and how hard he was trying, how bad he felt that most of his friends could read and he couldn't. The parents decided to meet with the teacher who then recommended an evaluation. They discovered their son needed vision therapy for a subtle vision problem and special reading assistance at school. The son was at grade level by fourth grade.

2. Integrity- Matching Your Priorities to Your Actions

Many parents give lip service to the importance of family life but don't devote much actual time and attention to it. Time given to the family on a regular basis,--not just for entertainment or fun but also for focused attention-- shows that you value your family life. Children are very good at detecting hypocrisy in their parents. Actions speak louder than words.

Paula and Frank sat down with their two early teens to talk about the danger of alcohol addiction. The only other Family Meeting had been to have "the talk" about sex a few months before. Their daughters sensed the awkwardness in both of these conversations which they interpreted as their parents not trusting them. The girls couldn't help but notice that Dad had a martini every night and several glasses of wine at dinner and that he either fell asleep in front of the television afterwards or picked a fight with their mom. They sat through the talk, said nothing and ignored what their parents said to them about the dangers of alcohol.

Sheila and Jack held regular Family Meetings. When their eldest started middle school, they asked him in their Family Meetings about school and occasionally they asked if he was seeing behaviors at school that he hadn't seen before. He shared with them that some of the 8th graders were bragging about drinking and drugs. This started a discussion about the family's values about the subject. From then on, whenever a parent had a glass of wine, the children felt free to comment about how this did or didn't fit in with the family's discussion about drinking. Over time, the subject was discussed several times at different ages and relating to other situations. The kids took in their parents values and even called them out when parents' actions were different than their stated views.

3. Preventing Problems

Family Meetings help the whole family become aware before an issue becomes a major problem. How? The topic could be raised in a Family Meeting, for example when there is a new behavior, or it may come up more naturally as a question about how things are going. By having a regular place that calls for noticing and bringing up topics, it is more likely that the issue can be resolved. Or if not resolved, caught early. Because the expectation is that everyone shares what is going on in his or her life, your child will be able bring up an issue that is just beginning—perhaps a bully at school or an invitation by a friend to engage in destructive behavior. Parents also raise issues at the beginning—mom going back to full time work, dad getting laid off. Discussing these real life issues and brainstorming together provides a model for problem-solving and for sticking together in tough times.

"My middle school child had more than the usual amount of homework on a busy weekend. She came up with her own plan! Her organizational skills have really improved."

"My nine year old boy will now do things the first time I ask!"

4. Countering Excessive Aspects of Popular Culture

Family Meetings are one way to counter the overwhelming influence of popular culture -- what our children's peers do or what they have. Family Meetings are a way to discuss and reinforce parents' values. For example, in a Family Meeting, the topic of wanting a particular item can result in a wider discussion. "How much is too much?" Participation in several sports and other activities all at the same time can be addressed to reflect parents' values about the balance of extra-curricular activities and schoolwork or the issue of health effects of too much physical stress or too little sleep.

Craig and Bill had no television at home, banned guns from their children's toys and made them accompany them on long hikes. They were wonderful role models of their own values but they never discussed or negotiated them with their children. Their son liked the same things they did but their daughter felt deprived most of the time. She began to spend more and more time at a friend's house where she could watch television and movies, try on clothes, eat pizza and pop. She was considered the black sheep of the family.

Elena and John were parents with priorities similar to Craig and Bill. But Elena and John held regular Family Meetings where they asked how things were going with friends and learned their children's views of what other families did. They had discussions with their children and were able to explain why they valued people more than things and why they saved money for family trips rather than spending it on a big television or expensive toys. They came to an agreement with their daughter about how much time she could spend at another home watching TV and the other activities she enjoyed.

5. Improving Communication Skills

When we listen and speak, we naturally improve our communication skills! This sounds obvious, but with our daily barrage of texting, emails, electronics, media and activities, we can inadvertently deprive our children of learning social skills and perhaps forget ourselves. When was the last time you spent more than five minutes listening, just listening, to a family member?

6. Changing Focus-- From Reacting to Cooperating on Developing Family Guidelines

What would Homer Simpson do? Let's compare Homer's approach with the Family Meeting model. Many parents would agree that they don't intend for their children to have as many toys and games as they end up having; the same goes for the amount of time their children spend in front of a screen instead of outside or with others. And surely you can think of many more ways that your actual parenting differs from what you intended.

So how does this happen and how can Family Meetings help?

I call it the "Homer Simpson Syndrome." You may recall a few episodes in which Bart pesters his father until his father gives in. The object of Bart's wishes could be a comic book or an Itchy and Scratchy movie. Whatever it is, Bart begins to parrot, "Can I? Can I? Can I?" until Homer gives in. Eventually, Bart just tells Homer he is going to pester him until he gives in so he might as well give in right now—and Homer does. Do any of you resonate with this story? At some point, if this or any other pattern is taken to an extreme, parents may wonder, "How did we get to this place?" They hate what has happened to their family life, to the way their children are behaving.

On the other hand, it also makes the parent feel miserable to constantly deny a child's sincere wishes. But wishes are not needs. When wishes are granted too often, they usually go against a strongly held value of the parent. I have often heard parents lament that the lives of their children are so different from what they had hoped. So what's a parent to do? Family Meetings are a regular way to look at patterns and to determine if they match priorities. Do we want to change our family rules or practices? Do we want to start new traditions that match our values? Family Meetings are the place to bring questions like these.

Family Meetings provide a place to make decisions as a family on more than just the current request from a child. For example, Marge Simpson would bring up the subject of how many outings Bart and Lisa can go to each month; both children would give their ideas but the parents would have the final say. Then it's up to Homer to remind Bart that he already had his share of outings for the month when Bart asks him. Doh! Family Meetings are a good place to negotiate and decide on guidelines for making decisions on how to handle specific requests.

Sound a bit sophisticated and time consuming? It isn't really. Think about it—how much time do you spend with the existing Homer Simpson pattern and where does it get you? Whenever parents complain to me about the time Family Meetings take, I point out that the time is an investment in the outcome. Ignoring a problem often results in more time spent on it down the road. Yes, I'm talking about the insistent, if not rebellious, teen. Haven't you heard stories of parents spending hours (years?) of grief and worry over their rebellious teen? Family Meetings are a way to include your children in rule-making and decisions before the teen years. This investment of time often avoids the time and worry of rebellion.

How otherwise would you have a conversation that goes like this, "One of the things I want to talk about in our meeting today is games. Some of the questions I'd like everyone's ideas on are-- how many games are enough, how much money we're going to spend on games this year, what games we could play as a family, and how much time is reasonable to spend on games to balance with our other activities. Let's come up with ideas. Who wants to go first?" A discussion follows, children have a say; their needs are considered but are not dominant. Parents can introduce boundaries within which the children can find solutions, such as the amount of money to spend or the amount of time games can be played.

How is this conversation different than the "Homer Simpson Syndrome?" First, the discussion reinforces the important difference between wants and needs. Secondly, children end up close to or on the same "side" as their parents. Children and parents learn to better articulate their opinions and priorities. The result is a "policy" or rule for the family as well as improved communication skills. The policy can be revisited when it needs changing. It can be revisited if it needs enforcing; this encourages both parents and children to follow through on agreements. And finally parental priorities are more likely to be lived out on a day-to-day, week-to-week basis by everyone in the family. While it might be stilted to talk about games in this way in our usual conversations, it seems very natural in a Family Meeting where any topic can be brought up for a focused and deeper look. I ask again, when else would you have a conversation like this as a family if not in a Family Meeting?

One workshop participant said, ***"I like the idea of saying 'yes' and would like to look for ways to say 'yes'. I am happy for the reminder of the difference between knowing and doing."***

How can a Family Meeting have a good spirit? What Spirit? How Family Meetings Are Handled Makes All the Difference.

"Family Meetings are a way to talk about things other than child's behavior." *Workshop participant*

Which would you rather experience yourself, a monotonous drone of talk covering routine subjects in great detail or a dynamic upbeat discussion of a few meaty topics? It's like the difference between the sound of fingernails grating on a chalkboard or the trill of a songbird, isn't it? We've all attended meetings that drone on. Let's create the other kind of meeting for our families.

If you've ever been to a meeting, you already know a lot about holding a Family Meeting. You know what worked well and what didn't. Family Meetings are similar to other meetings. The steps to holding a good business meeting apply to Family Meetings ***but they are not enough by themselves.***

It's not the steps of holding the meeting but <u>how</u> they are done that makes a good Family Meeting and builds a great family unit. If you take just one idea from this book, remember that foremost***, it's the way you, as parents, communicate that will make the difference.*** Adults may have a hard time at first remembering the difference between business or committee meetings where the focus is on getting something done and the focus in Family Meetings on getting along. This book will give you the communication skills and techniques to create a positive and rewarding Family Meeting and, over time, a wonderful family life.

Family Meetings are not like a weekly staff meeting you might have at work. No, what matters most is how *good* the meetings are rather than the outcome or how often they are held. Family

Meetings need not take up a lot of time; an hour or so every three months may well be enough. Like so many things in life, practice is what counts. The richness of family life develops over time. The spirit that grows, the sense of the family, the lessons learned about being there for one another, about listening and reflecting, problem solving and compassion—all of this is there for you if you are willing to stick with this simple process.

The spirit of the Family Meeting is the most important thing about it. What I mean by "spirit":

- the spirit of respect
- an openness to teach and to learn better communication
- the motivation to be close and loving to one's family members

All the steps that follow will not add up to much if the spirit of love and learning is absent. The steps are relatively easy; it's doing the steps in a spirit of love, of being on the same path in the family journey, that makes all the difference. It has for me. It will for you.

It's Quality, not Quantity That Matters When it Comes to Family Meetings.

Consider this-- there are families that hold meetings once a week, yet parents don't know what their children are thinking or doing; they have not established the kind of communication and closeness I'm talking about. In other families, the Family Meetings happen only when the parent or parents give orders to the children in authoritarian style. Also not a good thing. Were you part of a family that called a Family Meeting and your stomach sank, knowing one of the children was in big trouble? To receive a command from a parent? For scheduling? While the Family Meetings we are discussing in this book can address behavior, a sudden problem, scheduling and the reason why a parent feels compelled to issue an order, the main purpose of the Family Meetings in this book is to create a wonderful family life.

Many workshop participants have told me about the single time their family held a meeting when they were growing up. One parent's attitude was "my way or the highway." End of meeting. Others have recounted extremely negative Family Meetings. One mom recounted that when she was growing up, her father held a daily meeting to hand out the daily allotment of toilet paper. One workshop participant reported, "Growing up, if my father took me on his motorcycle and took me to McDonalds, I knew that it meant someone was dead or they were divorcing." Another family held weekly meetings but the parents never clued in to their daughter's early sexual and drug related activities. Yet another family met weekly, the only time they were together, to set the family's schedule, but never questioned the amount of time spent with the family versus the amount of time spent in front of a screen, with a ball, in lessons etc. They never attended to the challenges and changes in their children's lives or their own. This book will help you do better.

The Family Meetings Handbook is intended to help you create the close family that you want and that your children will cherish in memory when you're gone. This book is not intended as a means to help you plan your week, your menus etc., though you may use a Family Meeting for that in part. I am interested in something deeper. This book is intended to provide the means to create a family unit that can weather the hard parts of life. With a strong family, we can better resist many of the skewed aspects of our culture—too much time wanting things, too much time spent in front of a screen for both adults and children, too much work or too many structured activities. We can more easily focus on both the private and public good.

Parents Set a Good Example on Follow-through with Family Meetings

Holding a single Family Meeting is not hard, but doing them over time is a challenge. Motivation to continue with Family Meetings comes from truly recognizing their benefits. I have therefore included a great deal in this book on the purposes of Family Meetings.

Parents who have expressed interest in Family Meetings have often told me, "We tried a Family Meeting once." Parents give up Family Meetings for various reasons which we'll explore in chapter seven. Awareness of the obstacles is a start, but much more important are the ways to overcome these obstacles. Workshop participants over twelve years shared their ideas in this book just for you. Remember, families that hold Family Meetings over time, with an open mind and loving intent, build healthy, happy families.

Some Preparation Required

Yes, you need to examine where you, the parents, are coming from before you start holding Family Meetings. Take a moment to do the exercises, share them with your parenting partner(s) and you will set the stage for creating a wonderful home life. It takes just a few minutes and the investment will pay off in saved time and stress later on. You and your family can experience all of the many joys of Family Meetings too.

Most people will tell you that family is the most important thing in their lives. But do most people act as if this is true? Valuing family means putting time and effort into family life. You will be amazed at the difference Family Meetings will make in your family life!

It is my hope that you will take the information in this book and apply it in your own family. Parenting is a challenge. Many parents feel overwhelmed or give up and let things happen. I urge you to read on and to learn a process for parenting in an intentional and satisfying way. It's not hard to do. The opportunity is there for you to begin right now.

Here are some of the answers from workshop participants who were asked what surprised them in learning about Family Meetings.

"It was something I wanted to be able to do but felt it was a bit overwhelming; now I feel inspired and motivated and feel it is very do-able."

"Learning that the goal is to improve family relationships and communication, not the agenda items. That the meetings weren't all about problem solving and decision-making broadened my initial view and assumptions."

"The potential impact is far greater than what had occurred to me."

"I learned the importance of getting the children invested in the meetings. I will try to allow the children the opportunity to express themselves, and/or take charge of meetings."

"The opportunity to be so purposeful."

"It helped to hear other's stories and yet also good to make room for each person's story."

"I learned a lot from brainstorming the obstacles of continuing to hold Family Meetings and then problem-solving them."

"What surprised me was how open ended the meeting really can be and how it fits a niche in our family that I/we have wanted to communicate to and with our children."

"What surprised me was learning that the process can begin as early as age two!"

Stacey's Story

Stacey attended a Family Meeting's Workshop in 2005 when her children were five and seven. Even though her husband did not attend, he was willing to try Family Meetings and here is what Stacey and her family have to say seven years later.

"Our family was doing fine without any particular problems but I decided to take the workshop to become more pro-active in how our family would evolve. The workshop set the framework and I was able to push through my family's initial resistance. Solving problems as a family is so much better—we all have different needs. Often the kids are trying to learn something or do not understand something while the parents are "off" problem solving *for* them. Instead, we work with our children on problem solving together when that is what is wanted. We all listen to one another much better. And Family Meetings have spilled over into our family life and our lives. Our son, now aged fourteen, has become a confidante for his friends and I may be making a career shift that I would not otherwise have made. I definitely nag less since all I have to do is to remind the children of what was decided at our Family Meeting—or they will remind us, their parents.

Family Meetings give our children a way to voice needs. It often starts as a complaint. For example, our daughter was bothered by her brother reading the newspaper at the breakfast table, and sometimes Dad too. She brought this complaint to a meeting, not really knowing what was "wrong". The discussion broadened to, "What is family time?" and, "If something during family time bothers one person, it matters." Then everyone brainstormed solutions until a common one was found.

Our first Family Meeting was more formal than the ones we have now. We developed guidelines. They were simple—no getting up during the meeting unless it's for going to the bathroom, we'll speak in turn in a clockwise direction, we won't answer the phone during a meeting, we'll end with one positive item and we'll say something nice about one person at the end of the meeting. These rules stood us in good stead.

We have had a variety of items on our agenda over the years. We've discussed the details of our camping trips—we wouldn't have otherwise known that colored marshmallows would be a great addition. On a more serious note, we discussed how to spend an inheritance when Grandma died. The parents have the final say but including the children gave them a voice. Recently, sister was concerned about how much time her fourteen year old brother spent in his room alone rather than with the family doing things together. Previous inquiry resulted in monosyllables. By bringing up this issue in a more neutral way as the topic “I miss you, brother,” our son was able to share that he felt bored with what the rest of the family was choosing to do. Mom chimed in by suggesting basketball outside but sister wanted a board game instead. The family decided to find something that everyone would want. Dad got out his old Atari games one day and played with both children, something they all loved. Mom played Frisbee outside with the kids which they both liked. Another example is, at a much younger age, our son felt his Dad as scout den leader wasn’t treating him, his own son, very well. He was encouraged to sit on Mom’s lap and tell Dad directly about it in a meeting, a difficult thing for an eight year old to do. It turned out that Dad hadn’t realized he was behaving this way. Things changed for the better in scout meetings. In addition to enjoying more family time, we all learned not to make assumptions about why others act a certain way.

We have used Family Meetings to negotiate about homework and chores with little friction. We listened when our kids' voiced their need for no responsibilities after school until 4 pm and they listened and agreed to our needs to have chores done by 5:30 pm. There is no TV until homework is done. Yes, this came about after noticing that our children were starting homework after 8 pm or before school. We became more aware and then brought it up in our Family Meeting. There is no resistance to reminders about our agreement. And this is always an evolving issue as children get older. We are open to revisiting this and learn about the next stages and how best to handle them together.

It is surprising what items the children will bring up about their parents. Can you guess why the children raised an issue the solution of which was a curse jar? No one is dismissed for their ideas, feelings or values. Our meetings are a safe place to be angry, to cry, to share what you need to say and to ask for what you need. We learned a valuable lesson early on. When our then younger children would bring to the meeting the topic of mean kids on the playground, they had to tell us, “We don’t want your advice—you don’t have to fix it.” Wow! We have learned so much about contemplative listening. And this has spilled over to improve inter-spousal listening too.

In retrospect, Family Meetings have really molded how we treat each other all the time, not just in our meetings. It sets up a situation where everybody is equal and that’s not often the case in families; there’s often a lot of hierarchy. My value for giving kids a voice and having the light shine on them has carried over into my work life and my volunteer life as a way to further make the value I hold real. Family Meetings have built closeness in our family. We even argue better and our children argue well with one another.

"Yes, we still hold Family Meetings, though sometimes with a long gap in between. Our kids are excited when we say we will be having one. I think they feel it is an extra special space where they are really heard. We have solved several conflicts in meetings, so much easier to do when everyone is calm and listening, and many times it is the kids who come up with a solution. Sometimes we just talk about upcoming trips or get their input about ideas for summer vacations. It has been very worthwhile and I see it as an important means of communication as they get older and busier. Thank you so much for the workshop - 4 years ago for us now!"
Vanessa & Tom

A father took his children on the MAX light rail to a puppet show, having planned this outing in a Family Meeting. "It was nice to spend my limited time so well with my children!"

CHAPTER TWO: Parents Prepare for Family Meetings

<u>Exercise One</u>: **Your Starting Point is Important--A Snapshot of Your Family Life**

Before we embark on creating a happy, healthy family through Family Meetings, it makes sense to look at our parenting and family life right now. Are things going well and do you want to continue generally with the way things are? Is there more of a disconnect than you'd like with your family members? Do you parent well with your partner? Looking back in a few months or years, you can revisit this exercise to get a sense of whether you are happier with your family life and more on track with your goals as a parent. The survey will help you answer questions such as: "Are you really being the parent you want to be?" "Are you having the kind of influence over your children that you had hoped?" "What can be improved?"

This survey is also a great way to learn more about your parenting partner's point of view and to see how close it is to your own. Are you satisfied with your current family life? Is your parenting partner? If not, this can be the best motivator for beginning to hold Family Meetings. Are things going well and you want to continue with positive parenting? How will your family life evolve in the future as life and parenting get more complicated? Take this simple survey and then compare notes.

"With any activity, especially one as important as parenting, it would be important to engage in it in a mindful way and not just let things happen and react or overreact." Discuss with your fellow parent what you want in the children you raise when they reach adulthood. What values do you want to impart? There is a great variety- in addition to the more common ones. The French are always exposing their children to history and culture because they value it." *Giselle, French instructor and parent*

What do you and your partner value? Read on.

<u>Current Family Life Survey</u>: Parent One

1. As a parent, I aim to be here in the continuum from authoritarian to permissive (mark an "x")

Authoritarian..............................Permissive

2. I match my aim on this continuum…
Very well Fairly well Sometimes Not usually

3. I am satisficd with the family atmosphere that we have as parents and children in my family…
Very much Mostly Somewhat Not usually

4. My partner and I have discussed the messages and values we want to convey to our children…
Often or deeply Sometimes Rarely We plan to when___

5. I am satisfied with my influence as a parent on my child's values and activities; I have more influence than peers or popular culture…
Strongly agree Agree Not Sure Disagree Strongly disagree

6. How do policies get developed in your family? (policies around bedtime, food, siblings, chores, TV or computer games, homework, extracurricular activities, curfew, driving etc.) Describe the process as best you can. What are some phrases or words that come up when you think of this subject?

7. I am satisfied with the way we develop policies in my family…

Strongly agree Agree Not Sure
Disagree Strongly disagree

8. I am satisfied with how much time we spend together as a family…

Strongly agree Agree Not Sure
Disagree Strongly disagree

9. I know my family members-- their experiences, their preferences, their opinions, and their hopes and dreams

Very well Mostly
Somewhat Not really

10. What process is there in your family for dealing with problems or crises?

11. How satisfied are you about the process you have described?

Very satisfied Fairly satisfied Satisfied Dissatisfied

Current Family Life Survey:

Parenting Partner Two

1. As a parent, I aim to be here in the continuum from authoritarian to permissive (mark an "x")

Authoritarian…………………………Permissive

2. I match my aim on this continuum…

Very well Fairly well
Sometimes Not usually

3. I am satisfied with the family atmosphere that we have as parents and for our children in my family…

Very much Mostly
Somewhat Not usually

4. My partner and I have discussed the messages and values we want to convey to our children…

Often or deeply Sometimes Rarely
We plan to when___

5. I am satisfied with my influence as a parent on my child's values and activities; I have more influence than peers or popular culture…

Strongly agree Agree Not Sure
Disagrcc Strongly disagree

6. How do policies get developed in your family? (policies around bedtime, food, siblings, chores, TV or computer games, homework, extracurricular activities, curfew, driving etc.) Describe the process as best you can. What are some phrases or words that come up when you think of this subject?

7. I am satisfied with the way we develop policies in my family…

Strongly agree Agree Not Sure Disagree Strongly disagree

8. I am satisfied with how much time we spend together as a family…

Strongly agree Agree Not Sure Disagree Strongly disagree

9. I know my family members-- their experiences, their preferences, their opinions, and their hopes and dreams …

Very well Mostly Somewhat Not really

10. What process is there in our family for dealing with problems or crises?

11. How satisfied are you about the process you have described?

Very satisfied   Fairly satisfied   Satisfied   Dissatisfied

<u>Now Discuss and Reflect</u>

1. **Where do you and your parenting partner agree or differ?**
2. **How well do your respective levels of satisfaction with your current family match?**
3. **How do you see your family life evolving as your children grow?**
4. **What further conversations would be useful at this point?**

Messages and Beliefs: What We Bring to Our Parenting

You may wonder why this book starts by asking you about your "received" messages, beliefs, hopes and fears. We can't begin creating a wonderful family without looking at the parenting we experienced. It's that simple. Regardless of our best intentions, we all come to parenting with basic experiences from our own childhood and with beliefs that we have adopted or created. Parents are not a "blank slate." We all have had a childhood where we interpreted messages and beliefs from our parents, sometimes adopting and sometimes vowing to do the opposite. We often think that we will never sound like our parents or do what they did—until we hear ourselves doing it!

Most of us haven't thought about whether we want to continue operating out of these experiences or beliefs now that it is our turn at parenting. Let's take time to think about whether we want to create our own family according to our current values and beliefs as adults. We are not free to become the best parent to our children until we do. And when we do, we are then free to parent authentically and intentionally, without reacting to what we experienced as children. Family Meetings will help you follow through on the messages and values that you and your parenting partner want to convey.

Overcome your resistance! Many people have resistance to looking at their beliefs about parenting and to sharing feelings with their children. For example, if you were brought up with a lot of marital fighting, you may have concluded early on that discussing problems and issues is negative and results in no fruitful resolution. Or if you adopted a belief that "children should be seen and not heard" or "children are too young to understand or to deal with real problems," you may similarly resist these exercises as well as Family Meetings. Just do it! Look at your beliefs from the vantage of the adult you really are. The following exercise will only take a few minutes.

Another reason to do the exercise--we certainly can't know in detail about the messages and beliefs of our parenting partner unless we have discussed them. If you don't already know your parenting partner's response to the questions below, make sure that both of you spend a few minutes with the exercise; you will save a lot of time and conflict down the road. Be patient and share. You might just parent as a better team.

Examining Beliefs About Family

Let's get to the force that drives our actual parenting, the force that creates the messages we want to convey to our children-- our beliefs. These days there is no standard way to raise children. In prior generations, parents' beliefs were more uniform and strict than they are today. An example-- a widely held belief in the past was that children should be "seen and not heard." In Colonial times, American children ate silently, standing up at a bar and were excused as soon as they were done. Teaching children good manners was among the top parental obligations valued in the 19th century. Unlike a hundred years ago, today we accept a wide range of beliefs about parenting. So what is a parent to do?

Today most parents form their own beliefs, not usually from society's dictates, but from the parenting they experienced, media messages and perhaps unexamined thought. When we look at our beliefs about parenting, we can then ask whether these beliefs are realistic and valid. Do they set us up for a good family life or do they set the bar so high we will always feel our family (and perhaps we too) are coming up short? Looking at our highest ideals and beliefs also shows us how important our family and our family members are. We become motivated to be more intentional about our parenting. Take a moment to examine your own and your parenting partner's beliefs about parents, children and family life.

Exercise Two: **Family Meetings Beliefs Exercise**:

Parenting Partner One

1. What's your winning formula for happiness or for harmony in the family?

2. Write three beliefs or principles that you hold that would or have led to quality family life. They could begin with words such as "Parents will____." Or "Children are______." Or "A guiding principle I hold is or should be ____."

   a.

   b.

   c.

Exercise Two: **Family Meetings Beliefs Exercise**:

Parenting Partner Two

3. What's your winning formula for happiness or for harmony in the family?

4. Write three beliefs or principles that you hold that would or have led to quality family life. They could begin with words such as "Parents will____." Or "Children are______." Or "A guiding principle I hold is or should be ____."

   a.

   b.

   c.

Now Discuss and Reflect

- Examine or meditate on these beliefs or principles. Where did they come from?

- Are they as valid today as they were in the past?

- Are they held by your parenting partner?

- What do your children or your parents think about these beliefs or what would they think if they were more aware of them?

- Are these beliefs enough to create the family we want to live in and if not, what's missing?

What a gift you will give your children if, now that you are aware of the beliefs you each hold, you are willing to negotiate consistent messages to give your children going forward from the beliefs you do share! What a gift for your child to hear and learn what happens when parents differ on beliefs as all humans may do!

The A, B, C's of Parents' Beliefs

Here are some belief statements from workshop participants.

Parent **A**: "Have a nurturing parenting style with limit-setting too."

I grew up in a family where the parenting I got was not very loving. The rules were too strict and my brother rebelled. I want a better balance for my own children.

Parent **B**: "There are many elements for a balanced life for both adults and children. Balance your own needs and those of your children, balance work and play."

I grew up in a family where my father worked too much and my mother not at all and where academic excellence was the only way to succeed and win approval from both parents. That was fine for my sister but I struggled some with grades and had more trouble concentrating. What I was good at wasn't valued enough. I learned as an adult the value of balance for both children and adults.

Parent **C**: "Be a "good enough parent."

I see other moms spending so much time managing a "perfect" household and upbringing for their children that they lose track of the overall picture What they convey is either 1) not taken in by the child as loving or 2) is the hurried parent/hurried child model. I've learned that extreme self-expectations of the parent (or of the child) do not create a positive role model.

Parent **D**: "Respect goes both ways."
I don't understand parents who won't set limits for how their children talk to them—tone of voice and also the content. I see the negative effects of parents who don't demand some respect; it's not good for the children who, as adults, didn't learn what is acceptable to others.

Parent **E**: "Children want their parents' approval even when they say they don't or act like they don't care."
I remember how sullen I was as a teenager and yet how much I wanted my parents to be on my side. I wanted it both ways. As a parent, I want to reach the part of my teen that seeks approval while acknowledging why they are acting to assert their independence through behaviors that are obnoxious.

Parent **F**: "Children tune in to what we are feeling and also to any discrepancies between what we say and what we do."
Children are the best detectors of hypocrisy. For example, I learned as a child that my parents told

my brother and me not to drink but they always drank wine for dinner and often came home from parties roaring drunk. We were not allowed to comment when this happened. This has affected my brother more than me: he followed their model and has lost a marriage because of his drinking. For me, the lesson I got from my parents was about their hypocrisy. I want to be consistent in my behaviors with what I tell my children.

Parent **G**: "Positive reinforcement is better than negative reinforcement."
I was an elementary school teacher for many years before I became a parent. And luckily! I know from working with children in the classroom that positives are the way children learn best. Say every day to your children, "Today is going to be a great day." A few other things I learned as a teacher--separate behavior from the person; I will respect your developmental level, talents and capabilities; I will give you age appropriate responsibilities.

Parent **H**: "Our family is a team."
I grew up in a family that was more like four separate beings who happened to live under the same roof. As far back as I remember, everyone was preoccupied with their own concerns; there was no consideration or much interest in the others. In many ways, I feel I raised myself. I want better, now that it's my turn to have a family.

Parent **I**: "Parents are parents; children get to be children." We can be friendly but not our child's friend. My fellow parents often get this wrong and I want to do better. I have friends who befriend their children and rarely set limits. Their children aren't learning how to behave and it is very hard to be around them. Other parents expect their children to respond as little adults and don't take time to learn about the ages and stages that children go through. For myself, I want to be the parent and have realistic expectations that keep up with my children as they change over time.

Parent **J**: "One-to-one time for all family members is important."
I had the best experiences growing up when my father took me on a trip, just him and me. And then my grandparents took me on a trip and I really learned what they were like as people. I treasure those memories now and want to provide them for my children. Yet I want to convey that our family is a team and that every member feels a part of something bigger than themselves.

Parent **K**: "Everyone is as valuable as everyone else- it's not about only one person's needs."
It seems like too much energy is devoted to our child who is loudest and most demanding. I want to change this pattern. I don't think it's fair to our younger child and it's certainly seems a burden to us as parents. Each child is unique.

Parent **L** "No swearing, yelling and no triangles." [What's a triangle? It's getting someone else involved in an issue between two others perhaps to communicate for you or to ally with you.]
These seem such basic rules for getting along in a family on a daily basis. I grew up in a family of extremes—one parent was a strict disciplinarian, the other was hands-off. It was hard to be a child in my family. I'm going to focus on the goal of happy, well-adjusted adult life for our children. Parents will listen, everyone has a voice, parents decide.

Parent **M**: "I won't hold a belief about the superiority of a particular thing without checking my assumptions."
I have a tendency to pontificate. My children call it, "Getting on my high horse." Sometimes I think I know it all, and I forget to ask important questions about what a particular thing means to others, the intent or reason why they might want this. I want to change this behavior. My children tell me I'm a know-it-all. I want to change this way of being with my family.

Parent **N**: "Honesty and openness are keys to good communication."
I grew up in a family of secrets. My mother, I now realize, suffered from chronic depression. No one ever talked about it. I thought I was the only one who seemed to notice that she went to bed after

getting our lunches ready for school. She was still there when I got home! The elephant in the closet was scary. I never want to put my children through this. I think revealing oneself and speaking openly is the best way to have real family relationships.

Parent **O**: “Empathy is important.”
Too many times when I wanted to be understood, all I got was advice, especially from my parents! So I learned early on not to share my worries with my parents. They could never take the time to just let it be, to listen and understand and then to let me work on the problem or discuss it again when I was ready. With my own children I will ask, “What do you need right now, sympathy or solutions?”

Parent **P**: “Parents may hold contrary beliefs.”
I believe there is a tension between one belief that says parents will love their children unconditionally and another belief that a parent’s role is to teach appropriate behavior, respect and manners. Parents do get mad at their children. What if a belief of one parent may not be shared by the other? Some parents want adventure and surprise; others believe that structure and predictability is most important.

You may hold beliefs that are

Q,R,S,T,U,V,W,X,Y and Z:

The point is it's important for parents to think about their own background and their own chosen beliefs and then to share these with their parenting partner. Why is this belief-sharing important? To understand one another and work out how you want to handle differences between the two of you before you begin your Family Meetings.

What Messages do you want to convey to your children? When will you do this?

Messages:

We all received certain messages that were either helpful or harmful to us as children. And we all want to convey certain messages to our children. While it may be easy to come up with the messages we want to convey, it is hard to work them into ordinary conversation. That's where Family Meetings come in. When parents spend time thinking and discussing the messages and values they want to convey to their children, they are more likely to *actually* convey them. These messages are also more likely to be heard over the messages of a very noisy society when they are discussed in the special time of a Family Meeting.

Exercise Three: Family Messages Exercise:

Parenting Partner One

Write 1) the positive messages you actually received **or** 2) those you wish your parents had given you while you were growing up.
These are the messages that helped or would have helped you to feel valued and loved and those that helped you to feel confident that you could accomplish what you set out to do in the world.

1.
2.
3.
4.

Write down the messages you hope to pass down to your children. These can be the good messages and values you received while growing up or those you have chosen as an adult.

1.

2.

3.

4.

Exercise Three: Family Messages Exercise:

Parenting Partner Two

Write 1) the positive messages you actually received **or** 2) those you wish your parents had given you while you were growing up.
These are the messages that did or would have helped you to feel valued and loved and to feel confident that you could accomplish what you set out to do in the world.

1.
2.
3.
4.

Write down the messages you hope to pass down to your children. These can be the good messages and values you received while growing up or thosc you have chosen as an adult.

1.
2.
3.
4.

Now Discuss and Reflect On

1. How are you planning to convey these messages and values to your children?

2. At what age(s) were you planning to do so?

3. How have you done so far in actually carrying through on conveying these messages and values? (circle one)

Very well… Some messages conveyed… May have conveyed indirectly...Not conveyed

On the next page, look at what workshop participants came up with when they did this exercise. Consider their list when you are finished with your own. Bring forward those messages that are valuable to **you** in creating **your** family.

Sample Messages Parents May Want to Convey to Their Children

- Everyone gets time and attention in our family.
- Everyone contributes to our family.
- You will be independent.
- I will listen to you.
- We all look out for one another
- All of us can set goals.

"In one Family Meeting when our kids were teens, we put on the agenda two questions: 1) What do we want from this family? and 2) What do we plan to give? The most important answer was "belonging." The feeling of belonging is so central to families, yet so elusive to many and so problematic to others. Parents need this feeling especially as children launch their adult lives as ours were about to do. It was a gift to learn that

support and love were still wanted by our children at that stage and into the future. Another wonderful thing that came from these questions was that both children learned they wanted a good and tight relationship with the other as adults. And finally, the children expressed a continuing desire for a place to express their concerns. On the contribution side, our family members offered love, support and 'happy, peppy stuff.'"

Another topic that can be creatively addressed through Family Meetings is complaining. Complaining, often manifested through whining, can erode relationships and tempers. Parents think that only children complain. I have found it to be universal. And sometimes we just need to complain and be heard and acknowledged. We don't always need or want every complaint to be remedied and doing so is not a good life lesson. The complaints tend to escalate with the wrong kind of attention.

"As the result of a Family Meeting, we came up with something to post on the fridge for everyone's use. Across the top, it had a

column for the date (my children were 9 and 14), for the most common complaints and a column that said "I need acknowledgement". It had another set of columns under a heading labeled "To comfort myself I will…" This column had the most common ways listed to pull out of a down mood-- rest, exercise, read for a while, call a friend, etc. All a person had to do was put a check mark and initials. The interesting thing is that in the three months we did this, the column most marked was, "I need acknowledgement." Don't we all!"

- Others can have a different point of view than yours.
- Your family is more important. We value spending time with you.
- Step up to the plate i.e. take responsibility and don't wait for someone else to do it for you
- Be a good person.
- The Golden Rule- "Do Unto Others as You Would have them Do Unto You."
- Have concern for the world. Balance taking care of others with taking care of yourself.
- We have values about what's right and what's wrong.

"Different people are rewarded by different things. So, at the end of the meeting we asked what would reward each of us for doing what we said we would do. Here is the list:
Eldest child- an allowance
Mom- recognition
Youngest child- parent time
Dad- peace"

Examining Hopes and Fears About our Parenting and Our Children

What are your hopes and fears about your own parenting? What about your parenting partner? Workshop participants who have shared this exercise with one another discover that all parents have hopes and also fears about their adequacy as parents and the future they want for their children. Sometimes parenting can be a lonely business. Sometimes just knowing that we are not alone is helpful. Family Meetings offer an easy way to express our hopes directly to our children—and often a method to avoid our worst fears.

At a recent workshop, Bob shared with the

group his hope that his child would achieve success as an adult despite a severe learning disability. Examining that hope makes it possible for him to take steps to get his child the help she needs and to examine his own feelings in relation to his child's disability. It helped him to allow his child to fail and try again. Resilience is a wonderful parenting goal that came out of this exercise for Bob.

Another workshop participant worked in a hospital emergency room. His greatest fear was that one of his children would be severely injured like the children he has seen in the ER. He shed tears when he shared this with the group. Becoming aware of this fear helped him let go of some of it and will probably result in becoming less overprotective of his children or of his own feelings.

Please take time to do this brief exercise.

<u>Exercise Four: Hopes and Fears Exercise:</u>
Parenting Partner One

What are my highest hopes and greatest fears about raising my children?

- Highest Hopes
  a.
  b.
  c.

- Greatest Fears
  a.
  b.
  c.

What are some ways I can get closer to my highest hopes and avoid my greatest fears?

1.

2.

Exercise Four: Hopes and Fears

Exercise: Parenting Partner Two

What are my highest hopes and greatest fears about raising my children?

- Highest Hopes
  a.
  b.
  c.

- Greatest Fears
  a.
  b.
  c.

What are some ways I can get closer to my highest hopes and avoid my greatest fears?
1.

2.

Now share your answers with your parenting partner. Reflect on these questions:

1. What did you learn that you didn't know before?
2. What are some ways you can move toward your highest hopes?
3. What are some ways you can avoid your greatest fears?

Congratulations, you've done your part to prepare for your Family Meetings!

You and your parenting partner have answered some key parenting questions:

- **How satisfied are we with our family life and with our parenting right now?**

- **What do we want to share with our children, how and when do we want to do it?**
- **What do we want to model for our children and how do we want to do it?**
- **What do we hope and what do we fear about bringing up our children?**

CHAPTER THREE:

Answers to Your General Questions About Family Meetings

Q: What are the Purposes of Family Meetings?

A: Why would we want to take time from our busy schedules to hold regular Family Meetings? What would we accomplish? The purposes for Family Meetings are many: understanding the reasons you are interested in holding Family Meetings will motivate you to continue holding them. As already pointed out, it is holding these meetings over time that yields the benefits. Only through persistence can Family Meetings give the three most important messages—you belong, you count and you are safe in our family.

"Parenting can feel so all alone and then it's hard when there's a power struggle and I feel dumb in taking the bait. After taking the Family Meetings Workshop, I have renewed motivation to continue with Family Meetings."

Back to the question--there are so many purposes for Family Meetings! Take time to look at all the answers below. Workshop participants brainstormed them for you!

A regular time to connect. Keeping up with our changing lives, children and adults.

A time and place to make plans together and to bring up issues. To make sure small ones get heard.

To talk about expectations, needs and the ways family life together could be made better.

To demonstrate respect. To practice good communication.

To prepare children for independence by including them in decisions and later transferring control.

To show follow-through by meeting-planning-doing-repeat.

Q: What are the advantages of benefits of Family Meetings?

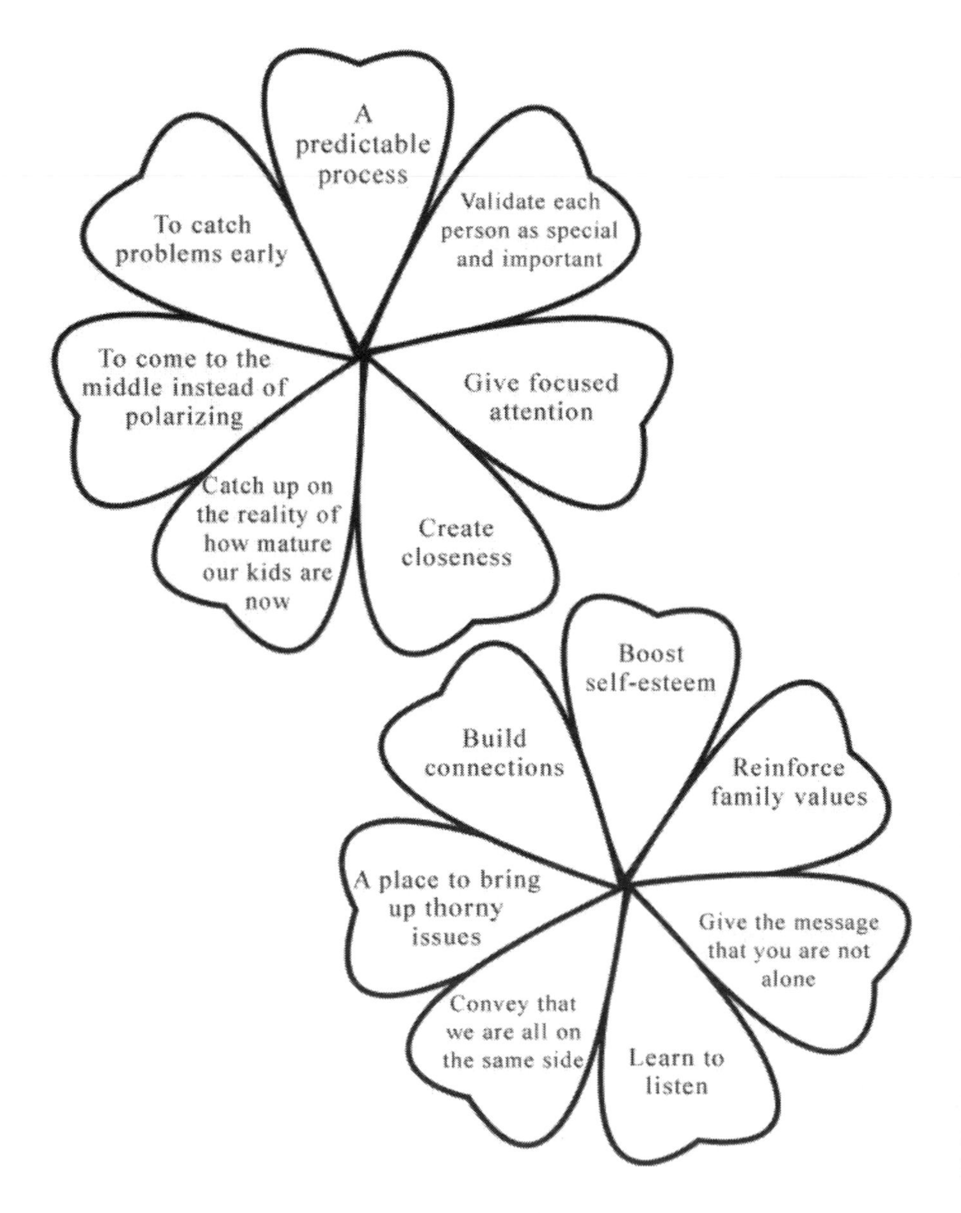

Q: What's the ultimate goal of Family Meetings?

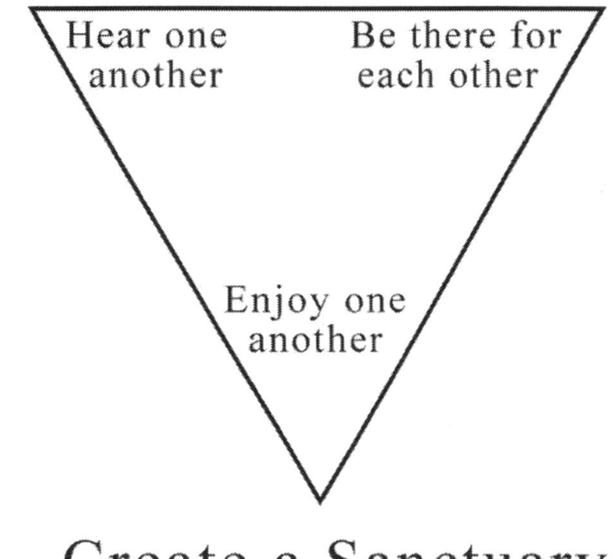

Create a Sanctuary

Use the workshop participant's brainstorm of purposes and advantages-- and your own ideas-- to explain to your children why your family is about to start a new tradition, holding Family Meetings.

What do kids have to say when they look back *at their Family Meetings?*

From an older teen. "Parents have a lot of power. It's a way to make kids feel they're being heard… People need to look at the question, 'What do I want to do?' It's a chance to ask, 'Is my life what I want it to be?' No one asks this and so many people are unhappy with their lives."

From another teen. "I remember negotiating my allowance. It was really cool that my parents would negotiate with me! I remember a friend who had very specific rules with no say regarding bedtime and allowance and she was jealous.

…[Family Meetings were] a way of bringing parents up to speed. Definitely I remember being treated like 12 sometimes when I was 14."

"It was good that my parents realized I could do my morning routine without nagging and then brought this up to give me recognition in the Family Meeting."

"It was good to have one fun item! It was nice to see that my family members all knew my interests and were able to brainstorm my 14th birthday party!"

"[My Family Meetings were] mostly warm and democratic. I felt nurtured and heard. Asking, 'How do you feel about that?' was a bit much but it was good to talk about feelings. In general it was handled really well. I'm closer to my family than most people my age."

More Answers to Your General Questions About Family Meetings

Q: How old do children have to be before we can start our family start Family Meetings? What's the best age?

A: The short answer is--as soon as your eldest child can talk. In my own family, our first child learned to speak early. By the time he was two and three quarters, he had developed his language skills and understanding well enough for us to have a short and simple Family Meeting. We had just one item for the meeting—how our child could become a big boy and sleep through the night. My husband and I realized how wonderful our Family Meeting had been and how respectful to have input from even very young children. Respect was and is an important value for both my husband and me. So we continued to have Family Meetings—for the next twenty years (note that none of the ideas actually resulted in our son sleeping through the night but the meetings brought us closer together.).

Q: What's the best age?

A: Certainly by the age of four, children are able and very willing to participate in Family Meetings. Families with several children four and under have had good experiences with their meetings so long as all family members are fed, rested and the youngest child (or an antsy child) has something to occupy his or her hands. The younger children may appear to be playing quietly but you'll be surprised when they pipe up with a comment.

 **Tip:**

Ages 2-4: When you begin Family Meetings with children aged two to four, keep it simple! Make it easy to signal the beginning of a Family Meeting, apart from other family time. Gathering in the same place with the same words or use a ritual that signals that this is the Family Meeting and here is how it begins.

"Children the age of two can't make big decisions like what to do if they have $100 to spend, but they can have a night a week of the week when they decide what to have for dinner. Biggest lesson I learned is to only give them choices when they really have a choice." **Family Meeting Workshop participant**

Q: When are the children too old to start Family Meetings?

A: The short answer is "never"—even adult children of elderly parents have used Family Meetings as a way to deal with the issues that arise as parents become infirm. But most parents that ask this question are having issues with their teen. The teen years are an especially difficult time to begin Family Meetings. Usually by the time a child is 13 or 14, the family dynamics are well established so that using a Family Meeting to change them is a real challenge. It is not impossible however; I personally know of families that have started or re-started Family Meetings at just this time in their children's lives. Here's one example:

Tom learned that his thirteen year old son drank alcohol to the point of intoxication at home with friends twice while Tom was at work. He was shocked; he and his parenting partner had a good relationship with their son and all indications were that his son would never do anything like this. The school insisted on an evaluation for possible addiction. After this was completed, the family began to hold weekly Family Meetings. At first his son was resistant to the meetings. In the Family Meetings, they planned outings that would be fun for him with the result that the family spent more time together. Eventually he dropped his friendships with the other teens who had been drinking and bonded more with his own family. Today, this young man is about to graduate from college and has a great relationship with his parents.

Tip: Children aged 11-15 may resist the idea of Family Meetings, especially if they perceive it as a top-down activity from their parents. Posting a place to write agenda items ahead of time is vital to signal to this age group that this is a time for them to bring items to the attention of parents. This is important even if they don't write anything down. Just be sure to ask for items at the beginning of the meeting. (See topic suggestion by age later in this book). Be sure to 1) ask open-ended questions, 2) use neutral topics and 3) listen more than talk!

Q: What do Children In Between Four and Eleven Like About Family Meetings?

A: Ages 4-11: Children of this age

understand the idea of Family Meetings as

the opportunity to influence rules and activities. They are often the most enthusiastic participants and sometimes the most challenging in terms of sharing time and using “I” statements. (see Setting Ground rules).

Tip: Pick a time for the first several meetings.
By scheduling several meetings, you set the expectation for yourselves that you are starting a new tradition in your family, one that will continue over time. Family Meetings will help you create the family you’d like to live in if you do them over time.

Q: How do we know what to talk about?

A: See Chapter Five for a detailed answer by children’s ages. But the best way to figure out the items that family members want to talk about is to ask. Post something in plain view for family members to jot down agenda items. If your children don’t yet read or write, ask them what they would like to talk about in the time you've set aside for a Family Meeting. Ask ahead of time and write their ideas down for them.

Here's an easy way to gather the topics for your meeting or for the first few meetings.

Post This Something Like This On Your Fridge

Situation in which things went well	Situation in which parent annoys child	Situations in which child annoys parent or one another

Q: What are some topics for Family Meetings with very young children?

A: Here are some suggestions:

1. Agenda item with a three year old: "How can Mommy and Daddy Have a Pleasant Dinnertime?" Again, this very young child had ideas! They included his being excused as soon as he was done and playing nicely nearby. This resulted in a pleasant dinnertime for all and an added incentive to continue Family Meetings. After just a few reminders of what the family had decided in the meeting, the child knew what to do at dinnertime.
2. Food: One of my workshop participants, Sherry was quite frustrated by her four year old daughter's eating habits. She was only willing to eat four foods. Sherry and her husband told their daughter that they would soon be having their first

Family Meeting and asked their daughter if she had something she wanted to discuss. "Yes," she said. "I want to talk about 'yummy fruits.'" When they held the Family Meeting, the decision was a trip to the grocery store to try some new yummy fruits! The parents were thrilled that their child brought up the subject of variety in foods herself and that they were about to have a wonderful family outing to choose new foods for the family. What a win-win!

3. Planning a family outing. Not all Family Meeting topics need be about resolving the prickly side of family life. Even two year olds can tell their parents where they would like to go or what they would like to do. The negotiations around the outing (the where, when, how to make it fun for all) teach give-and-take on the part of both parents and children.

Tip: Practice with these easier topics so that your family is ready to tackle more meaty subjects later on. For example, dessert is a good topic to revisit from time to time over the years and one that allows for a discussion of values, listening to one another's point of view and working together to create a "policy" that meets the most wishes of the family. It's also an opportunity to follow through once decisions are made about dessert--a relatively easy one compared to teen driving, for example. You might even make the dessert together!

Q: "Family Meeting" is such a dry name, it reminds me of work. Do we have to call it a "Family Meeting"?

A: Many people complain about the name "Family Meeting." They say "It sounds so artificial." "This isn't a business." "I never could hold a meeting with my family." "I have to have meetings at work; no way do I want to have them at home."

It doesn't matter what you call it. You can call it something that sounds more like fun or give it a family code name; you can even call it, "Ralph". The point is to provide a regular place and time for important discussions in the spirit of love over a period of time, no matter what you call it. (If you find that someone in your family reacts to the word "meeting" you might try "family forum" or "family council." Find a name that suits your family; one workshop participant suggested "pow-wow." Personally, I prefer "Ralph!"

Q: Why would we want to hold Family Meetings if we only have one child?

A: Setting aside a special time and place to bring up issues, to check in with each other, and to plan ahead is still a vital part of maintaining a healthy relationship with your child. With one child or one parent, issues around too much involvement and too much absence are likely. With an only child and two parents, your child may feel like he or she has no input because it's always two against one from the child's point of view. Family Meetings are a good forum to find out one another's views and change the 2-1 dynamic. Listen. Talk. Brainstorm and teach your child how to think and talk about issues.

Q: What if there is only one parent?

A: Single parenting is harder and setting aside the time to meet as a family will be harder. It's even more important to have regular meetings as a way to stay current and to brainstorm the many issues that will inevitably come up. Many frustrations can be addressed before they explode!

Q: Do we need Family Meetings if we have a lot of family time on an everyday basis? We have dinner together almost every night.

***"I discovered that dinner table conversation doesn't really do it. It's a relief to talk about issues when no one is angry."* Workshop participant**

A: This answer has several parts:

Part 1: Many people tell me that they don't need Family Meetings because they discuss everything at meals. I am not present at those meals, but I suspect that there is the dynamic of what I call **"statement-bam-distance"** around the table. To illustrate, imagine a child asking to go to an event that he or she really wants to attend but which raises concerns for the parent. The parent, after little discussion, responds negatively, the child argues and distance is immediately created. The **statement** is, "I want to go to this event." The "**bam**" is the parent's answer, "no." and **distance** is created. Discussion tends to be shortened or polarized around the dinner table. Another illustration of this dynamic occurs when the parent suggests a solution to a problem the child is having at school and the child gives reasons why it won't work; distance is created. In our family, we recognized this dynamic and gave it some humor. When I anticipated my idea being shot down quickly, I asked my children to get their "gun" ready and they would make their hand into a pretend gun and "shoot" the idea down. We would laugh and then sometimes we could have a serious discussion about what was underneath the suggestion or concern.

Dinner conversations tend to limit thoughtful decisions, to skip over addressing and validating the feelings and concerns of the participants and many of the other intentional elements that are present in Family Meetings. D**iscussions in a Family Meeting are special conversations**.

Part 2: Dinner conversation often results in the quieter members not participating much and then not getting the message that they count and they belong. Many times in dinner conversation the more chatty family members consistently bring up subjects and the others do not. Around the dinner table, there is no one making sure that everyone brings up items that are important or that the time is shared. “What happened at school today?” is a frequently asked question. It often elicits a very general response or one that emphasizes only the positive parts of the day or tells some information about another child. “Johnny punched Jed while on the playground.” Same for a parent’s sharing of his or her life. The child does not usually ask about the parents’ life during dinner. And as with children, the quieter parent may not share much.

Part 3: As I have said in the workshop, *“Emotions are fine, but not when we dine.”* Dinnertime can be a place to discuss world issues, for example, but for families, the items that need discussion and resolving are often the emotional/social ones. Do you really want to address hard issues over a nice dinner? Think about the hard subjects- sex, drugs, illness, death, moving, or divorce. Would you bring these up over dinner? Would you want tears at the table? The truth is that almost everyone will avoid the hard things in order to avoid a stomach ache; those that continue may get "negative attention" as a result of continuing the conversation. Is that what you want at the dinner table?

Part 4: Dinner conversation is different than discussion in a Family Meeting. Ask yourself how often you listen deeply, reflect, brainstorm and plan with the intent to follow through on decisions made at the dinner table. Does dinner conversation feel like special time where anyone can raise something on his or her mind? Is dinner where decisions can be made for more than the one thing that needs a decision right now? **Hold conversations about how your day went over dinner. Save Family Meetings for times when hunger and tiredness won't interfere with longer, thoughtful discussion.**

"Family Meetings open the lines of communication. They are less confrontational

than we experience in dinner discussion. Often [at dinner] we have a shorter conversation which is more about conclusions and opinions than dialogue and true understanding."

"Family Meetings are pro-active, not reactive."

"Family Meetings address the thorny issues. To talk about things we wouldn't ordinarily talk about, those things that might cause tears if discussed at the table."

One mother reported that "When I left my job, my eight year old told us in a Family Meeting that he was concerned there wouldn't be enough money. He was comfortable enough to say it because we had regular Family Meetings. We might not have known otherwise. And then we could reassure him. This is an example of something that was nipped in the bud."

Q: What if this formal way of meeting doesn't work in our family?

The answer to this question also comes in two parts.

Part 1. Some people think a more formal meeting is too contrived. What if we changed our thinking and substituted the word “intentional” for “contrived” or “formal?” It’s all in the way you think of it. Intentional parenting is deliberate without being contrived. Then it makes sense-- if we have an intention for a certain kind of family life and loving relationships, we can create this life through deliberate and regular Family Meetings.

Part 2. Be creative. Try a meeting in your car on a long drive. The car has the advantage of less eye contact which may make it easier to reveal the burdens of one’s heart or mind. Have shorter meetings that are less formal; spice them up with throwing a nerf ball to the next person when it is his or her turn to speak. One workshop participant rotated meetings in each of the kids’ bedrooms so they would feel more comfortable. There isn’t one right way to hold Family Meetings. Family Meetings are different than meetings at work!

Tip: Workshop participants reported that 1) having the meeting in child's bedroom made things more "cuddly" 2) having the meeting at the kitchen table rather than in the dining room, made it more clear that Family Meeting was a separate, specific and special thing and 3) having the meeting in living room allowed youngest child to roll around on floor during meeting which was okay for everyone. So feel free to be creative!

Q: This is just one more obligation I have to check off my list, so why do it?
A: It sounds like you've already decided that Family Meetings are a burden and not the wonderful experience they often are. It sounds like you might think that Family Meetings are not worth the time. Try a few and I bet you will learn something about your children's lives that you otherwise wouldn't have known. Or you may hear mature wisdom from your child that you wouldn't otherwise have heard.

Make Family Meetings pleasurable so they don't feel like yet another obligation. Be sure to include the fun topics! Why not end your meetings with a game or a great snack. Make the meetings yours. And speaking of burdens, think about what a burden it will be if you will be dealing with teen issues or young adult independence issues because you didn't take the time for Family Meetings now. The time you invest now will pay off many times later on. I attest to this myself.

Q: Do Family Meetings really work? They are mostly about process, what about results?

A: Yes, Family Meetings work. They are not the only way to have great outcomes for children and adults but they are a proven way. Family Meetings may be more efficient and complete than the informal ways that parents use instead. Not only do I know this from personal experience, but also my workshop participants report back that Family Meetings have made a huge difference in their families. There are lots of positive results. Families decide together on rules, vacation or holiday topics, getting along together, getting schoolwork done, friendships and then all of the not-so-nice issues that come up in family life- deaths, illness, sexual norms, and more.

"Grandpa died suddenly in his sleep yesterday. The parents and their children have held Family Meetings for several years. They know what to do. They have a Family Meeting. Mom asks if each person can say how they are doing with Grandpa's death. Their eight year old daughter, with a tremor in her voice, says she is wondering where Grandpa is right now. Their eleven year old son asks what usually happens after someone dies. The parents do their best to answer these questions honestly. Then Dad explains that Grandma, his mother, never would go to funerals, which is the ritual most families have after someone dies, and that she is not planning to have one for Grandpa. He asks the children if they should have a ritual for Grandpa. As the discussion continues, the family decides to buy a memorial tree to plant in the yard and to ask their minister to come to their house to lead the family in honoring and remembering Grandpa. And so it was. This happened in my family with my children." KF

Q: We had a Family Meeting once and we never got anywhere. Why should we keep on having more?

A: It sounds like you wanted resolution of a problem or a decision on an issue. In Family Meetings, there has to be a balance between getting things done and getting heard. Here are some tips for helpful ways to keep this balance:

Getting heard:

Just getting heard is often the most important aspect of Family Meetings. So keep in mind that some topics are being aired just for sympathy or understanding. Action is not always required. Ask the person who raised the topic what they want or need from the discussion. You may be surprised.

Often a person who doesn't feel heard or acknowledged will repeat him or herself. It is helpful for the meeting leader or another family member to paraphrase or guess at what the speaker means before going on to the responses of others.

Otherwise the meeting may end in frustration, going over the same ground.

Tip: The meeting leader can also avoid getting into a pattern where one person tries to convince others by repetition. He or she can point out that the argument was heard and understood, by getting nods and then saying, "Now we're moving on."

Tip: The meeting leader must make sure that the time is shared. This should be one of your ground rules.

Getting things done:

It's always a balance to involve everyone in a decision and yet wait until the moment is right-- to pay attention to those who have said little along with those who are impatient to move on or have made up their minds. Sometimes delay by one person creates a bad feeling. It is the role of the meeting's facilitator to lead the topic toward decision within a reasonable time but not necessarily within one meeting. Use the benefit of regular (and possibly a special meeting) to come to conclusion on topics.

Tip: Here's some language you might find helpful to push things along.

- **"I think everyone has had their say on this topic. Can anyone summarize briefly what each of us said?"**
- **"Are we ready to talk about solutions or are we too tired or tired of this topic to decide right now?"**
- **"If we don't decide right now, can we agree to decide first thing in our next meeting?**

Q: What if my children don't like Family Meetings?

A: Some kids say they don't like Family Meetings. One of my own children told me this every meeting for years. Nevertheless he attended the meetings willingly and often brought his own topics; when he turned eighteen he thanked me for all those Family Meetings! Some kids will test your resolve about holding meetings. Your determination matters. If children sense that you might stop having them, some will surely take advantage. When your child either says or does something about his or her dislike of Family Meetings, it is another opportunity to reinforce how important they are to you as parents. Remind your child that it is his or her time to influence how things go in their family or with their issue. This is the time, this is the place.

Q: What if my parenting partner doesn't want to continue Family Meetings?

A: There may be many underlying reasons for his or her opinion. Find out what is behind their statement. Is it a feeling of not knowing how to do this new activity? Is it a fear of being challenged or questioned? Of having to examine their own emotions or reasons? Of feeling inarticulate? Of having to follow through?

If one parent won't participate in Family Meetings, there is no good solution. Proceeding alone gives a divisive message to your partner and to your children. Foregoing Family Meetings is a loss for the parent who wants to do them and perhaps a loss of the ability to parent as a team. See if you can work out a compromise, perhaps by holding Family Meetings less often. It is not the frequency but the quality of these meetings that matter.

Stories from workshop participants:

"Our family had great success with our meeting because we asked our 3 year old to bring a comfort toy. Dad then told how his day was. Mom asked Dad if he had any questions. The meeting brought up an issue that the family didn't know was brewing and one that would have grown into something bigger a few months down the road. It was the issue of how to have both a family vacation and a family visit with relatives next summer. The issue isn't resolved but it has had two rounds of discussion and will be addressed again."

"Our family held two brainstorming Family Meetings recently. We brainstormed about charities that the family would donate to at Christmas time. We learned about several charities, shared the information and selected two that all agreed were the ones to give to. The other

meeting was to brainstorm day trips for summer since there wasn't time for a family vacation. We took two of these trips and have the list on a white board for future reference."

A third family recounted a Family Meeting in which they used a tangerine as the "talking stick." "The tangerine was colorful and you could easily see who had the family's attention. There were two items on the agenda- how the school term went for our fourth grader and Christmas presents. The first item went very well because she is doing excellent work and is so much better organized than previously. She was so proud. We parents were able to see her and each other as individuals in this setting rather than in the usual chaos of day to day life.
On the subject of Christmas presents, when I suggested the idea of doing Christmas presents as I'd read in an article on how to simplify Christmas, our daughter got upset and ran upstairs. The proposal was to choose three gifts-one thing you need, one thing you don't need and one dream. The child saw the three gifts as limiting but we parents were able to explain, when she came back to the meeting to work things out, that the "limit" was about how to make the gifts more meaningful and thoughtful and not to "limit" the number. The meeting ended well. In fact, the gifts looked like a lot more

than three under their tree because other relatives sent gifts too."

Another workshop participant learned that their child wanted to know about how to interrupt parents' conversation. Parents learned they need to give some space between comments to let this happen!

From a divorced parent of a four year old. "My partner, my son and I had a Family Meeting just a few weeks ago that was just great. We kept it short and fun, and we came up with a fairly simple list of "family rules" that we have posted on the refrigerator. They include serious things that we all agreed to, like, "We treat each other with kindness and respect," "We all help with the cleaning," and "We have a family celebration at least twice a year." But we also came up with funny ones like, "No singing like Bob Dylan," and "No farting in the kitchen, unless you're alone." We joke around a lot about violating those last two. Since we all devised this list of family rules together, my son is totally in favor of them (they're his rules too), so I think this is a very good thing for him and for all of us. Since my ex and I are still on such good terms, we will probably have Family Meetings that include him in the future so that we can all stay in the loop on what is best for our son... I thought you might like to know that your

workshop was good for us, that we still have Family Meetings, and I think we probably will forever."

"I remember in particular a helpful bit of wisdom from our children. As we were struggling with the financial pressure and seriousness of putting a child through college and also dealing with the emptying nest, our son observed and daughter agreed that what we parents needed was to have more fun and to act more spontaneously. We heard it, took it in and began to take our children's advice!" KF

CHAPTER FOUR:
Nuts and Bolts on How to Hold Successful Family Meetings

How to start and how to do Family Meetings. Don't worry, it's not rocket science.

Q: My partner and I have done the preparation to begin holding meetings. Now what do we say to our children about them? How do we tell them we're going to have a Family Meeting?
A: For young children, you might say, "We're going to have a special family time where we talk with each other about how things are going, questions we have, anything bothering us. We're going to have our special family time on Saturday when Mommy and Daddy are home, after snack time. I'm going to put a piece of paper on the fridge so you can tell me things you'd like to talk about when we have our Family Meeting, and I'll write them down for you." Make clear that everyone in the family will have a chance to suggest topics to talk about.

For children over four, you might say, "We're going to start having Family Meetings where we can talk about things. Anyone in our family can suggest what they'd like to talk about. We'll find out more about what is going on with each other and we can plan family outings or talk about things that bother us. Is there anything you'd like to bring up that you can think of right now? If not, there'll be a paper on the fridge to write down our ideas and you can always ask me to write one down for you. If there are a lot of ideas, we may not get to them all the first time but we'll be having these Family Meetings time every few weeks."

Talk about the fact that, as parents, you want a closer knit family. Explain that you want to set aside time for learning about your children and vice versa, that this is a chance to make decisions and plans together, to discuss important things, to ask for and to give each other encouragement and to talk about what family means to you. **(See the Purposes section above.)**

Q: How long should our Family Meetings be?

A: No more than an hour and considerably less for young children. Our family started Family Meetings when our son was still two. Our first several meetings were about ten minutes long and had two items, the second one was always planning something fun.

Tip: If your family generates too many topics, congratulations, you've done the agenda for several meetings! If there are a lot of backlog issues that are more urgent, try having Family Meetings more often to catch up.

One workshop participant's family decided to do a fun activity together directly after their meetings. Everyone looked forward to playing games together afterwards. The children were patient through the 45 minutes of the meeting and then had a fun evening. They got to play simple games like Yahtzee, Life and Sharpshooters with their parents; they were left remembering laughing and having a good time right after their meeting.

Q: How can we make the meetings "good" for our family?

A: Take time to do the "What You Already Know About Good Meetings" Exercise! Start with what you already know. Take a few minutes to do the following exercise with your parenting partner.

<u>Exercise Five, What You Already Know About Good Meetings</u>: Parent One

Imagine a meeting, class or workshop that you thought was well run or was particularly satisfying. When you've gone to a particularly good meeting, what made it good for you?

1.
2.
3.

What things did the leader of the meeting do to make you feel comfortable, included, heard?

How did this person or another keep track of the time and the agenda? Was there a separate scribe?

How did this person make sure that people participated?

How were decisions made? How were they tracked during the meeting?

How did the meeting end?

How can you apply these ideas to your own Family Meetings?

1.

2.

Exercise Five, What You Already Know About Good Meetings: Parent Two

Imagine a meeting, class or workshop that you thought was well run or was particularly satisfying. When you've gone to a particularly good meeting, what made it good for you?
1.
2.
3.

What things did the leader of the meeting do to make you feel comfortable, included, heard?

How did this person or another keep track of the time and the agenda? Was there a separate scribe?

How did this person make sure that people participated?

How were decisions made? How were they tracked during the meeting?

How did the meeting end?

How can you apply these ideas to your own Family Meetings?

1.

2.

Here is what workshop participants said about what we already know about satisfying meetings:

- *They are structured/organized*
- *They are in service to the meeting's purpose*
- *The leader keeps the group focused and respects the member's time*
- *Everyone listens and talks with attention and respect*
- *The meeting allows for quiet and talkative members to share time*
- *The meeting leader identifies whether the conversation is for expressing feelings/thoughts (clarity), generating options or for making decisions*
- *They're interactive and collaborative*
- *Decisions feel good to all (even those who have compromised)*
- *All points of view are heard*
- *While facilitating, the meeting leader does so without a particular point of view*

- *The group helps people articulate what they are trying to say and uses examples*
- *The facilitator is confident*

Tip: Eat and then Meet

A Family Meeting is hard to have on an empty stomach. Family members tend to be short with one another when hungry or tired; they tend to have less patience for listening or for probing beneath what is said to discover the intention of the person.

Tip: Be aware of your tone of voice and your attitude –and those of others around you. Keep in mind that the spirit of the family is being created through Family Meetings.

Remembering what we already know about satisfying meetings, we're ready to learn what's unique to Family Meetings.

Q: What are the steps involved in holding Family Meetings?

A: Here's an overview. Let's go through all the steps and then go back through each one in more detail.

1. **Collect topics for you Family Meetings**
2. **Welcome and each person briefly says how they're doing**
3. **Decide who is the leader of the meeting and who writes the important things down**
4. **Decide on the meeting's agenda of 2-4 topics**
5. **Address each topic**
6. **Restate and write down decisions (and ideas for later meetings)**
7. **Try to arrange trade off among topics or decisions. Model compromise.**
8. **End the Family Meeting with a positive agenda item**
9. **Ask each person how the meeting went, note improvements for next time**
10. **Follow the meeting with something enjoyable**

Step 1: **Asking for topics** for the Family Meeting allows the unexpected to happen. Both before and at the beginning of the meeting, ask each family member for agenda items. You would be amazed at the items children will bring up, if asked.

One parent recounted. "In our first Family Meeting after the workshop, my son shared an incident that happened from kindergarten that I never would have learned about if it had not been for our Family Meeting. The incident would have been 'stuffed' inside my son and could have been the basis for forming a belief about himself."

Asking each person in the family for topics shows respect and creates an expectation of suggesting an item before the next meeting.

Tip: Use neutral language for each topic. Often a topic is voiced as a complaint. For example, "I hate my brother!" The meeting leader needs to find neutral words for the topic—it's really important. So, how do you neutralize a complaint? Here are some examples:

- **“I hate my brother!” becomes “How can younger and older brothers get along better?”**
- **“No one does chores around here, it’s a mess!” becomes “How can we all do our share of the housework?”**
- **“I have no friends!” becomes “What’s going on with your friendships?”**

You get the idea, right?

Step 2: Welcome and reporting in. Begin the meeting with a **welcome**, a “check-in” on how each person is doing today (or another family ritual you choose to begin your meetings). These should be short. If you have trouble keeping it short, you can suggest thinking of reporting in as a type of weather and then asking for each person to say their personal weather (and just their weather—with no explanations). It works!

Step 3: Choose a leader and a **note taker** for the meeting. The leader’s role is to make sure that everyone has a chance to speak, to make sure that guidelines are followed (no interrupting, for

example) and that the topics are either addressed or set aside for the next meeting.

Tip: Same old, same old is fine. It doesn't matter whether the leader is always the same person or is rotated among family members so long as the basics are followed. And it doesn't matter if one person has both roles, though children who are eight or older appreciate taking an active role.

Step 4: Set a simple agenda- no more than four items; for young children just one or two. If there are more than four suggested topics, so much the better—you'll have the agenda for the next few meetings.

Tip 1: At the first Family Meeting, the first item for decision is what are the ground rules for these meetings.

Tip 2: Parents should feel free to put items on the agenda that are typical concerns for their children's age group and also to include items about their own lives. (See Q&A on topic suggestions by age below). Encourage your children to raise topics for the meeting.

Step 5: Address each topic. How?

a) Clarify the topic – ask questions, listen, ask clarifying questions, listen again.

b) Ask for family member's feelings about it. Sometimes the person can name the feelings but other times not. Parents can help by suggesting how someone in that situation might feel and asking if this is how the person who raised the topic feels. (Parents can ask about, but should not assume, the feelings they think may be present.)

c) Acknowledge the feelings behind what is said. All feelings are okay but not all actions. Keep in mind that often acknowledgment is all that is needed on a topic. We don't need to solve our children's problems or anyone's for that matter.

d) If it seems appropriate, talk about the values or priorities you hold in relation to the specific topic. Don't lecture. Remember when you were a child and your parents lectured? Resist the temptation.

e) Brainstorm, if appropriate (be careful not to comment on or say something negative about ideas in order to keep ideas flowing)

f) Decide on action when the time is right through a process that fits your family, such as consensus, modified democracy, or choosing between acceptable alternatives. Don't rush to decisions or delay so long that family members are frustrated.

Step 6: Restate and record decisions-this is a check for everyone's clear understanding and can be referred to later.

Step 7: Try to arrange win-win situations. You can use more than one topic to accomplish a win for everyone. For example, an agreement to reduce the level of sibling bickering can be used as a way to "earn" a fun family outing or vacation.

Step 8: End with a positive agenda item. Why? This is how everyone will remember the meeting—positively!

Step 9: Ask how the meeting went for each participant. (What did you like, what did you wish had been different? What surprised you?)

Step 10: Follow with something enjoyable – a snack, games, family hug or a family ritual.

Overall Tips:

1. **Remember it is good to check in with one another on very basic, common issues for each age, including adults. Parents should feel free to put items on the agenda that are typical concerns for their children's age group and likewise to include items when they need or want more family support (work or life issues) for themselves.**
2. **Make sure everyone knows that the purpose of the Family Meeting is to set aside more family time and to have discussions; similarly make sure everyone**

knows that the Family Meeting is not a result of bad behavior or a particular problem.

3. **Create an expectation that Family Meetings are enjoyable. Ask where each person would like the meeting to take place, if this is appropriate. Ask what would be an enjoyable way of ending these meetings.**

The Seven Elements that ensure that Family Meetings keep the tone and spirit that builds our family

When we hear the words "Family Meeting", we tend to focus only on "Meeting" and forget the other word--"Family." In a business or volunteer setting, our focus is on getting things done. For meetings with our family, we want to focus on creating closeness, respect and communication. Keeping in mind that the spirit of the family is being created in, as well as through, Family Meetings, make sure that each meeting includes the following **seven elements**:

1. Creating a welcoming and safe atmosphere

2. Talking about values in relation to situations

3. Improving communication skills- active listening and taking turns talking

4. Separating feelings from the person who has the feelings and also from behavior. For example, it's okay to have strong feelings but it is not okay to act them out by hitting.

5. Focusing on problem-solving only when you feel that everyone is ready.

6. Creating a sense of unity and belonging

7. Never lose sight of the goal-- providing a safe space for important conversations.

Remember, you're creating the family you want to live in!

Q: What do you do if one person talks too much or another one doesn't want to talk at all? How do you share the time?
A: You know your family members best. If one is extra talkative or extra quiet, start with an open-ended question for everyone to answer in turn for 2-3 minutes. For example, let's each share how things are going with our friendships for 2-3 minutes. You can set a timer or ask someone to track the time. This is a good job for the most talkative family member. If someone doesn't feel like sharing, they may feel more like it if they are last, perhaps agreeing with what someone else said. Encourage but don't force the issue. In discussing ground rules, you can address how your family will share the time, including the option to "pass" on a particular topic.

Tip:

Encouraging phrases for the reluctant participant

- **"We haven't heard from you yet and we'd really like to know what you think."**

- **“Is it more like this for you or more like that?”**
- **“Some people would feel or think this under the circumstances, is that what you’re feeling or thinking?”**

Encouraging phrases for the talkative participant:

- **“We’d love to hear more but it’s time to turn to…**
- **“You have such interesting things to say that I’m sorry to cut you off right now. We’ll talk more about this next time or after the meeting.**
- **“Can you summarize what you wanted to say because we only have one minute left for your turn to talk.”**

Q: Ground Rules: How can we create that safe space for conversations? At the first Family Meeting, of course we want to agree on some ground rules. What are some of the basic guidelines for meetings?

A: The guidelines set the tone for the meetings. Everyone has input on how the family members relate to one another, perhaps for the first time. Guidelines prevent common problems in meetings. They can be referred to when the meeting gets off track. Most meeting leaders find that when we pay attention to expectations for behavior from the beginning, the content takes up more of the meeting rather than dealing with behavior. This, in turn, makes the Family Meeting more satisfying.

Guidelines come in several categories; the decisions on them come from your family.

1. **Respect**- Nothing is more important than treating one another with respect in a family. The Family Meeting should be the model of this behavior, one that continues into day-to-day family life. Some guidelines that promote respect are 1) no interruptions by people or devices 2) everyone has an opportunity to speak 3) no name calling.

2. **Confidentiality**- what does the family want shared or not shared with others? What rule will create a safe time and place for sharing?

3. **Focus on listening**. How will we accomplish this best? What about distractions? How will we make sure that we listen first, then speak? Even questions in the midst of a person's sharing can redirect or misdirect the focus of what they are trying to say. How will we focus on listening?

4. How will we make sure that **everyone gets a chance to participate**? How will we share the time? Some families use a time keeper, others use a "talking stick." How will we make sure we use our time for speaking wisely?

Tip: There will be times when the focus is more on one person in the family. It's the meeting leader's job to ensure that other family members have their turn in most meetings and that one person doesn't dominate the meetings.

5. What are the **meeting leader's "rights**?" The leader of the meeting has the responsibility to

make sure the meeting has the elements of good meetings already discussed (validation of feelings, participation, sharing time). The leader needs to have the right to interrupt and to bring back the discussion to the focus and to move through the agenda at a pace that's comfortable for most.

Tip: Keep in mind that, in Family Meetings as in life, we do not expect perfection; we all make mistakes; we all are teachers and we all are learners. It's hard for the meeting leader to remember all of the good listening, sharing and respect ideas during the thick of a family discussion. And same goes for all family members.

Workshop participants suggested and then used the following guidelines for their Family Meetings.

- *Confidentiality-what is said in the room, stays in the room.*
- *Everyone needs to be there*
- *Keep an open mind*
- *Be creative*
- *Lighten up*
- *No labeling and no put-downs. Ex: "You're a ___!"*
- *Everyone has a chance to talk; agree on how to share "air time."*
- *Practice listening*
- *Check-in. We will have a time to just tell things, time to be heard*
- *End on an up note*
- *Before brainstorming, we will paraphrase issues and feelings.*
- *A child sets one agenda item each time.*

- *Speak from your own perspective. Use "I" statements.*
- *Don't bring up "old stuff"—focus on current items or bring up the old stuff as an item in itself.*
- *Appropriate "fidgets" i.e. things to keep a child's attention but no gadgets that take away attention*

Q: Why one positive item at least?

A. Negatives are easy to identify because they stand out or annoy us--it might be Suzie's grades or Johnny's video game time or the family chores not getting done. We all know what is going wrong and may focus exclusively on those items if we are not purposefully reminded to have at least one positive item. These items may constitute the whole agenda. What a downer! Who would want to continue meetings like that?

A good rule is to require at least one fun item—planning a family outing, someone's birthday, or a summer vacation. In my family at one meeting, we talked through the elements of what each of us wanted in our summer vacation and then decided on two volunteers to plan each day and make the reservations. All the family had to do while on vacation was to follow the plan. Great fun! And a great experience in how to organize and plan for both children and adults.

" Lots of families have meetings only around negatives. … My kids light up at the prospect of having a meeting where they have their say and have continued to love Family Meetings. My kids remind me when the meeting is scheduled." **SN**

Q: Why write decisions down—it seems so formal?

A: Experience speaks here- if someone doesn't write it down, the family either will not remember or will remember several different versions of the decision. Writing down what is decided and who will carry through decisions is important. First of all, it helps establish effective communication. There are so many opportunities to miss the meanings or to think you understand the meaning when you don't. Secondly, it is not uncommon for a decision to be made but each person thought another person would carry it through or do it in a different way. Writing it down allows everyone an opportunity to see where there are gaps or later, where the miscommunication occurred. It can avoid blaming and arguing about "who said what." Writing it down provides a way to follow through, an important lesson in itself for both parents and children. Put the decisions on the refrigerator or bulletin board for all to see. You won't regret it.

Tip: Communication consists of at least six parts: 1) what the speaker means, 2) what the speaker thinks he says, 3) what the speaker says 4) what the listener hears, 5) what the listener thinks he hears and 6) what the listener understands. Communication is a lot like the child's game of "Telephone." Checking for understanding is an important skill in Family Meetings.

Q: Why are regular Family Meetings so important?

A: While they don't have to be particularly frequent, Family Meetings should be held regularly—that's how they become that safe space to bring things up and to make the connections with each person over time. Family Meetings are often something everyone looks forward to. Your family isn't going away. Build a family you want to live in, one where you keep up with your children's changes and your own.

"My kids are not afraid to tell us what they want or what they need. And they are more aware than most of the difference. The more opportunities to talk with our children in a meaningful way, the better."

"I feel like we are in a lull with our parenting right now but the teen years are just around the corner and this tradition of communication will be invaluable."

"We have improved our communication skills. For example, Dad's a better listener now."

Q: I tend to be literal and react to the words people say. And then argue about them. How can I do better?

This is an important question. **Please read Chapter Eight on communication** for a more in-depth look. But here is the quick answer-- slow down your own reaction to the words and ask about why the person said what they said. Go behind what is said to find the intent. Communication is a learned skill. The first step is what is said. Going deeper involves finding out what was meant and what feelings underlie what is meant. Recognize and check your assumptions with the person who is speaking. Be patient with yourself—it's a learning process. And feel free to acknowledge to others when you have reacted or over-reacted. Apologies go a long way.

Q: In this "me, me, me" world how can our family make different decisions that are more in line with our real priorities?
A: Practice making decisions in your meetings based on needs and concerns rather than wishes and desires; an important part of social learning is to figure out the distinction. Without thinking more about what our real needs or concerns are in any given situation, we can't think clearly about whether or how to go forward with priorities.

More details on the Steps to Successful Family Meetings:

Q: What are the Four Types of Topics for Family Meetings?

"My family brainstormed topics for a Family Meeting when our eldest was eight and our youngest was three and a half. Here is what our family came up with: 1) recycling 2) television time and sweets 3) helping others 4) sharing and 5) keeping on track. Interesting!"

A: There are four general types of topics for Family Meetings:

1. **Situations that arise from current family life.** Most often, the topics will suggest themselves, sometimes with much urgency. You'll have no doubt that the issue needs to be addressed. Often these situational topics remind us of a larger issue or of other situations; they can result in family rulemaking.

2. **"Keeping up" types of topics.** The "keeping up" types of topics have to do with regularly checking in on each person's well-being. For children, this is often as simple as the topic of how we are doing with friendships; for parents, it is often how we are doing with work. As children grow, we parents tend to think of them as younger and more immature than they really are! Keep up.

3. **Hard issues**. Whether from family life or the topics that parents often have trouble bringing up (sex, alcohol and drugs etc.), Family Meetings are a good way to bring up hard issues. In my own family, in addition to the death of a grandparent, we addressed the serious illness of a parent, malicious behavior by classmates, boyfriend/girlfriend issues, our family's teen driving rules, planning for college, family finances and much more.

4. **Planning**. Everything from planning for fun in the future to "our family's values" can be part of

your Family Meeting agenda. You may be surprised by the things your kids will say!

Tip: It is important that Family Meetings include all four types of topics over time. Why? Because Family Meetings aren't just about problems, they are about encouraging one another, knowing one another, making age-appropriate family decisions and becoming closer through regular deeper conversations.

Q: How should we handle things when emotions run high in a Family Meeting?
A: There are several options. 1. Someone in the meeting stops the rising voices. 2. The leader should note that the level of emotion is getting too high for comfort. Then ask what the family wants to do. 3. Parents always have the right to table an item so that emotions can cool. That is the wonderful thing about Family Meetings—they aren't urgent decision- making sessions called to address a particular situation. So there will be time for another discussion. Hooray! In fact, you can discuss how to deal with the high emotional level

next time, refer back to the ground rules, or ask what would make each family member feel more comfortable with this topic when it comes up next time. 4. Another option is to reach out to hold or hug the family member who is upset. Sometimes that's all that is needed and wanted. I speak from experience here—sometimes I have given and sometimes I have received hugs and a lap in the middle of our Family Meeting.

CHAPTER FIVE:

Ages and Stages of Childhood Development: Suggested Topics for Each Stage

As parents, we need to learn about the general development for children at each stage so that we can match our expectations with our child's abilities. We can't expect a four month old baby to talk or walk, right? Below, I've included basic information about ages and stages and how these relate to Family Meetings. Check it out and see what you think.

Here's one example: ***Argument with a four year old over bedtime. Dad agrees to "five more minutes," not realizing that a four year old most likely has no concept of "five minutes," even if she knows the words. She is likely to believe that when the time is up, there will be more negotiation similar to the one that just occurred and so will beg for five more minutes. When the five minutes are up, the child argues for five more minutes, the father says "no" and, reminds the child of the agreement. The child cries. The father attempts more explanations. Finally, the child, exhausted (remember, it's past bedtime) yells, "Stop Talking!" The father then carries a crying child to bed. Lesson—even an articulate child is usually within the general developmental stage of his or her age!***

The other aspect of “ages and stages” is that every stage has both an upside and a downside. Many books have been written about development in children. The following is a brief summary of some of the information. I have included Family Meetings topic suggestions for every stage. Of course, your family will address the topics that come up in your life. Family Meetings focus on more than problems. The suggestions here are a resource for you when you are looking for a positive topic for your Family Meetings or one related to keeping up with your changing family. The suggestions may also prove useful in creating new family traditions, enjoyable family time or keeping abreast of how each person is doing and what each person is thinking. Getting to know one another and keeping pace with ever-changing lives are some of the many benefits of Family Meetings.

Birth through 1 year:

Upside: child develops trust from prompt response to his or her needs. Child smiles and coos and has increasingly long periods of focused attention. Child is able to attract attention with smiles as well as tears.

Downside: Child needs 24 hour care and supervision, may awaken frequently at night, and begins to teethe, which is painful. Child is irritated. Cries. Child typically begins to catch viruses.

One to Three Year Olds

Upside: Child explores, discovers, walks, learns, understands simple concepts and begins to talk. Child makes many associations and has a sense of wonder. Child makes sense of his or her world.

Downside: Child doesn't know what's dangerous or, even while "knowing," wants to test parental limits. Child's behavior deteriorates when hungry, tired, sick or teething. Seeks a lot of parental attention. Can be oppositional (known as the "first adolescence"). Very energetic. Needs supervision. **Family Meetings:** From about two and a half on, parents can initiate a short Family Meeting. Some families have incorporated a brief ritual such as lighting a special candle and sitting on the floor together. The parent can address a need or desire of the parent such as, "How can we have an easier time getting going in the morning?" You will be amazed that even children as young as two or three will come up with ideas!

Ages three to five

Upside: Child is able to cooperate and is learning to share. Child learns symbols such as colors, shapes, letters and numbers. Child's language increases dramatically. Generally cooperative and imaginative. Masters many large motor skills and some small motor skills.

Downside: Short attention span and many distractions. Very energetic. Problems with transitions from one place or activity to another. Still learning parental limits and still needs supervision.

From workshop participants:

"We've been having Family Meetings since your workshop. It's been amazing. It feels like we have a kind of partnership with our daughter (aged 4)."

Our child remembered all the agenda items even though he couldn't yet read!"

"If I hadn't tried Family Meetings with my five year old, I wouldn't have thought he would be so good at it. I'd have waiting until at least 10 years old."

"Our eldest child raised the topic, everyone playing with his toys. Then the other children said they had this problem too, often from him, the youngest. The kids worked out an agreement to ask first and respect the answer and rules of use for the toy requested. This has made a huge difference. The kids have

worked out many agreements about using each other's toys. There is less anger between them."

Family Meetings:

Encourage the child to come up with a topic. Often it will be one concerning time with a parent, food, toys or an outing.

Brainstorm ways to make the morning or evening routine better.

Talk about holidays, birthdays or grandparent visits.

Ages five to eight

Upside: Children learn to read and write. They play with one another and are often quite social and imaginative. They want parental approval and rccognition. They are figuring out the social structures, games and rules. They value fairness.

Downside: they may resist structures and test limits—by lying or otherwise. They can be mean to one another and sometimes to parents.

Family Meetings:

- Plan how the family would like to celebrate holidays or one particular holiday.
- Address the family tasks and how each member contributes to the household. Allowances can be part of the discussion or a separate discussion.
- Children's friendships, how are they going?
- Children's sibling relationships, how are they going? Ask how the parent can help, if any help is wanted. (Parents can discuss how important it is to them that their children love their brothers and sisters, especially when they are grown up. Often this never gets said!)
- What is most important to each family member about being in a family?
- Screen time- what is enough? What is enjoyable about screen time? Why do

parents have concerns? How do parents model behavior in this area?

"In our family, we created two new holidays. One was 'Ice Day' where we agreed to collect hail and snow in the winter and to store it in the freezer. Then we would get it out on 'Ice Day,' the hottest day of summer. A second holiday was 'Candy Day.' This grew out of parents' concern about the frequency of eating candy every day instead of more nutritious food. On Candy Day, the children were given a certain agreed on sum of money, they shopped for the candy and had to eat whatever of it they wanted in one day." JH

"My kids initiated a chore chart and my husband and I contributed. Now we have expected chores, and chores worth points which can be converted to money once a month. We haven't done this for long, but my kids are very excited about doing chores now. All is not perfect, but I think we've achieved more empathy for each other and are striving to treat each other better." S.N. children 6 and 9.

Ages eight to eleven:

Upside: Building skills in every area. Greater understanding of the world and of relationships. Longer attention span. More independent. Activities outside of school. Interested in parental approval and involvement.

Downside: Pseudo-sophistication, talking back, sarcasm, insistence on having their way so they can "fit in." Peer pressure. Friendships can be all-important. May be overscheduled.

Family Meetings:

- How to keep the family closeness when children are involved in sports or lessons?
- Plan the family vacation within parameters such as time and money.
- Parents' values and expectations around alcohol, drugs and perhaps sexuality. Ask what children would like to know.
- How is school going for children? How is work going for parents?

- How is the balance with extracurricular activities, practicing, homework, family and friends?

A real life example: A parent initiated the topic of the parent's own lack of mood control at times in a Family Meeting. The kids gave ideas and now know that they are not the cause of these outbursts. The parent gave a good message by owning the problem and avoided having her children believe that they could never measure up and that's why the parent got angry. The parent took responsibility for her part and the children for how they contributed to outbursts.

Ages eleven to fourteen:

Upside: Greater independence and maturity. Learning organizational skills. Greater awareness of social scene. Interest in the opposite sex. Establishing identity.

Downside: Adolescence! A desire to fit in can

lead to peer pressure and testing of limits. Hormonal and social pressures lead to emotional overload. Sarcasm and anger at times.

Family Meetings:

- How are children feeling about their rapidly changing selves, the problems they now see around them with other kids, their desire to be like their peers? (Parents can share some of their memories from this time of life. This topic acknowledges that things have changed and is an opportunity to ask about how these changes are going.)
- Discuss the possibility of a coming-of-age event and if so, what it will be.
- Plan a party, either for the family or for the children. Birthday parties can be a wonderful cooperative brainstorm.
- Plan the schedule for summer. Some children need a lot of stimulation and others like quiet time. Parents need to feel that their

children are supervised. Discuss these needs and how they can be met.

- How to change past routines such as bedtime, morning routines, after-school activities, curfew, and unsupervised time.

Here's what another mother had to say about her Family Meeting topic of chores in this age range.

"The whole buy-in process of working it out together gives each child more ownership of how they want to function in the family. Although not perfect, it is a lot less frustrating than the alternative, and as the result we've been successful in keeping an 11 1/2 year old and almost 14 year old on track, with a lot less hassle. Imposing a system generated by the parents, without the Family Meetings, would have met with a lot of long-term resistance and resentment. As it was, we just had resistance and resentment about having the Family Meetings. We've been reaping the benefits ever since, making it a small price to pay." **LT**

Ages fourteen to seventeen:

Upside: Greater maturity, less need to fit in. Establish individual identity. Skill development continues. Learning foresight and planning. Greater independence and responsibility. Needs less hands-on supervision. May not show it, but wants parental approval.

Downside: Need for independence may outstrip judgment and parental limits. Testing new behaviors and self-images. Must deal with societal issues such as sexuality, alcohol and more. May not be willing to plan ahead in ways that affect the teen's future as an adult.

Family Meetings:

- How you, the parents, envision your adolescent as an adult and how they see themselves.
- How your adolescent wants parents to behave around his or her friends.

- Family slogans and sayings.

"In a Family Meeting when our youngest was a freshman, we parents made our expectations clear—not 'You need to get an A or else' but rather, 'We want you to succeed, finals are new to you, they take more effort and study than you've previously had to do, we are here to listen to your plan for studying and we want to plan with you the extent of our help with your process.' Together, we came up with a mutually agreeable plan. It turned out she had some fears about her first finals and that she did want our help to quiz her on the material, to go over it with her. She did well on her first finals and was encouraged. She also didn't get all A's and wanted to do better the next time around."

Topics that workshop participants have addressed in their Family Meetings for children in this age group:

Death of a grandparent

New expectations and new freedoms

What we each like for leisure

Getting along better with older teenager

Parental worries and how to deal with them
Kids' worries
Planning for fun: Birthday Party, family outings etc.
Expectations while visiting relatives- anticipating solutions for problems
Strengths of each family member, one weakness
What to say to me when I'm upset
How to deal with too much activity
Plans and expectations for foreign students' visiting
Kid's feeling like they don't fit in at school or have no friends
Finances and college

CHAPTER SIX: A Sample Script -- How does the first Family Meeting actually go?

Let's imagine a family of two parents and two children, ages four and six. Here's a possible (and perhaps idealized) script for how the meeting would go.

After lunch, mom says,

"Okay, everybody, it's time to come into the living room for that Family Meeting we talked about. I have the paper from the fridge. Who wants to bring a stuffed animal for us to hold when it's our turn to talk?"

Once gathered, a parent says,

"Welcome everyone. Let's turn on this special light for our special family time. Dad, do you want to turn on the light? Let's start with just a few words on how life has been for each of us lately? Sara, do you want to go first?"

The welcome and checking in with one another should take no more than 10 minutes. Tips for keeping this part of the meeting short, if you have a very talkative family member or more than two children--use a checking-in question such as "tell me in one breath how things have been going for you lately." Or you could set a

time and a timer. Remember, this is just a chance to say something, not to start a conversation about what the person has said. Just listen!

Continuing on with the meeting:

Mom says, "Who wants to make sure we follow the topics we chose and share the talking time?" *Let's say that Dad volunteers.*

"Who will write down what we agree on? Who will keep track of the time? We want to keep our meeting to 45 minutes."

Let's say that the eldest child volunteers to watch the time. He or she may need reminding.

Tip: Don't force family members to take roles. It is fine to have one person with all roles, especially at first.

Dad says, "Okay, we're ready to start by setting the rules for our meetings, just like you do at school and we do at work. What guidelines or rules would be good to have in our Family Meetings--rules about sharing time, making sure we all have a chance to talk and to listen? "

The guideline part of the first meeting is very

important. It may take up to 20 minutes to talk through the "do's and don'ts" rules for Family Meetings. You may have the chance to experience interruptions and distractions that help you with rules. Revisit the rules you've made if they are violated at the following meeting. Be creative. If someone can't sit still, suggest something the person can hold that will keep their hands busy so they can listen better. Adults often use knitting or note taking. Children often use a stuffed animal or silly putty.

Think about these questions for the "rules" part of your meetings.

Confidentiality*- what does the family want shared or not shared with others? What rule will make the meeting safe for sharing?*

Focus on listening. *How will we accomplish this best? Should we have a rule about turning off cell phones? What about other distractions?*
How will we make sure that we listen first, then speak? Even questions in the midst of a person's sharing can be distracting.

Participating. *How will we make sure that everyone gets a chance to participate? How will we share the time? Some families use a timekeeper, others a "talking stick." How will we make sure we use our time for speaking wisely?*

There will be times when it is appropriate to ask the family for more time for one person.

Meeting leader responsibility*. What are the leader's "rights?" The leader of the meeting has the responsibility to make sure the important elements of the meeting happen (participation, sharing time and acknowledging feelings). How can the leader exercise these "rights?"*

Learning. *How do we convey that we do not expect perfection? We all make mistakes, that we all are teachers and we all are learners. There is no one right answer.*

Continuing on with the meeting:

Dad: "Here's what Mom wrote down last time about what we agreed are the rules for our Family Meetings. We can always change these if we don't need them or if we need more of them or if we need to be more creative with them. Let's talk about this again after a meeting or two and see how they work, okay?" Everyone nods.

"Now let's get to the items we wanted to talk about. Let's see what we have on this list from the fridge. Whatever we don't get to today, we can talk about next time. One thing for sure, we should end with a topic that is something fun. Let's talk about one other topic and then talk about this one here on a fun family outing next weekend and save the rest for next time.

Tip: no more than four topics in one meeting even if you're "on a roll."

Dad: "I see that someone isn't happy about some messes we've had around the house lately. Was that your suggested topic, Mom? Where do you think our family is with neatness?"

Tip: Make the topics as neutral as you can; the language above is much more neutral than, "This house is a mess!" And more appealing than the topic "chores."

Instead of stating the topic as a problem, state the positive and desired outcome. For example, instead of the topic of "meltdowns at dinnertime", use the agenda item of "How can parents have a pleasant dinner?"

Instead of just venting frustrations about too many or too late snacks, have the agenda item "snack timing experiment" and use it as an

opportunity for learning and for using that learning to develop rules that meet all the important needs of both parents and children. Consider broadening the topic from a child's request, "Can I go to this event?" into a more general discussion of the parameters for permission for events (how much advance notice, values around the proposed activities and their cost). With regular Family Meetings, you won't be caught at the last minute to decide on requests one by one.

Continuing on….

Dad says: "Kelly and Leslie, can you tell us how you see things about neatness and messiness in our house? ….Mom?... And here's how I see it…..

Dad says: "Mom, I see that you have strong feelings about this. Can you tell us more about what you feel and what you think when you have those feelings?"

Mom: "When I come home from work and there are toys are all over, I get frustrated and angry. I think to myself 'No fair! It's more work for me when I'm already tired and I want to relax and enjoy being with my family. I resent being the main person picking up toys that I don't leave out.' And then I sometimes yell at you or some of you. I don't feel like playing with you by the time I've cleaned up the toys and the dinner things. Then I get sad that I'm missing out on good times with you."

Dad: "Kids, can you talk about what you just heard from Mom? Did you understand what she said?.... Can either of you tell me what mom is feeling? What does she think when she's feeling that way?"

…

Dad: "Mom, did we understand everything you said? Did we get it right?"

Kelly: "I don't want to spend all the time cleaning up!"

Leslie: "I'm too tired! And besides, it's Kelly that leaves out all the toys!"

Dad: "We'll get to that part too but can you first tell me what you heard about Mom's feelings and thoughts? What were they again?"

Kelly: "I heard mom say she's angry and tired when she sees our messes. She thinks it's 'no fair'."

Leslie: "I didn't do anything!"

Dad: "But what about Mom, was she angry at you in particular?"

Leslie: "I don't know. I think she was."

Dad: "Let's ask her."

Mom: "No, I'm angry at the situation that all of you don't seem to notice the mess and I can't stand it when I get home. So I end up cleaning it up and then getting too tired to do anything enjoyable. I'm not angry at any one of you, just frustrated. I'd like this house to be comfortable for me too."

Dad: “I’d like to say something about what Mom said. I didn’t know that all these feelings and thoughts were going on for her. I didn’t know how strongly it affected her and the way she interacts with us on work nights. I don’t have these feelings myself. I guess I have a higher tolerance for messiness. All I knew about messiness around here was when she yelled and then we all scrambled to do something to clean up. I feel bad that she gets upset when she gets home from work. I’m sad she doesn’t have time or energy to enjoy family time on work nights. I feel a bit guilty for not noticing the messes around here until she says something. How about you, Kelly, how do you feel about what Mom said?”

Leslie: “I feel bad. Mom gets angry and I think it’s because of me. I get a little scared when she yells. And then I talk back and she gets really mad. But I get tired by the time Mom gets home too. I’m a person too!”

Dad: “I hear you.”

Mom: “We’re all tired then, aren’t we?”

Dad: “And you, Leslie?”

Leslie: (crying) “I don’t like this talk.”

Dad: "I see it upsets you, Leslie. Can you tell us about it?"

Leslie: "No."

Dad: Would you like to come on my lap?

Leslie: "Yeah."

Dad: "It looks to me like we're too emotional to work on the neatness/messiness around here. What would you all think about bringing ideas to the next meeting about how we can help mom be more comfortable when she gets home from work? Does that sound good? Can you wait, Mom?"

Mom: "Sure. I feel better just having said it and gotten you to all to understand my point of view."

Kelly: "Okay."

Leslie: "Sniff, okay. But I don't want to cry next time!"

Dad and Mom: "Hug time, okay? We love you both. (Group hug)"

Dad: "Now for the fun topic. Who wants to suggest a family outing for next Saturday?"

Tip: When you are planning a family outing, discuss what would make this outing fun and then address what might interfere with the fun and how to deal with what might interfere.

Kids: "I do, I do!"

Dad: "Leslie, how about you tell us first."

Leslie: "Now I forgot it."

Dad: "Okay. Let's hear from Kelly and maybe by then you'll think of it again."

Kelly: "I want to go to the zoo!"

Leslie: "I don't want the zoo, I want to go to the swimming pool!"

Mom: "I want to go visit Grandma."

Dad: "I want to go to the beach."

Dad: "Well, we have four great ideas here. Does anyone have a suggestion about how we'll decide?"

Mom: "How about we do all of these ideas but decide today on the order of them?"

Kelly: "Hooray! Four outings! I like it!"

Leslie: "But I want my idea first."

Mom: "I have an idea. We should look at the weather for next Saturday because a few of the ideas are much more fun if the weather is good. Let's see, I have the forecast here on my phone. I'll turn it on and get it."

Kids: "Okay, mom."

Mom: "Next Saturday it's going to be rainy and cool."

Dad: "So that leaves going to Grandma's or going to an indoor pool. How about we each vote on these two ideas and see which one is the winner."

Kelly: "I vote for swimming!"

Leslie: "I vote for Grandma!"

Dad: "How about you, Mom."

Mom: "Well, visiting Grandma was my idea and I still want to do that. We haven't seen her in a long while and I can see in my mind how happy she'll be if we come."

Dad: "Well, it's close for me but I'm going to vote for Grandma and save the swimming for the next time which can be either rainy in which case we go to an indoor pool or if it's nice, we can go to an outdoor pool."

Mom: "We've been meeting for about forty minutes now. I'd like to end our meeting pretty soon. Three out of four of us voted for the visit to Grandma so that's our decision for the first of our four outings. "

Kids: "Me too, me too."

Dad: "Okay, today is Saturday and we've planned our outing to Grandma's for next Saturday so how about we meet every two weeks for a while?"

All: "Okay."

Dad: "So we'll still have the paper on the fridge to write down ideas for what we want to talk about. Let's get ready to turn out our special light. Kelly, can you turn off the light? And can we end our meetings with a cheer like 'All for one, one for all'?"

Leslie: "That's pretty corny, Dad, but I guess it's okay if you don't tell anybody outside the family."

Kelly: "Yeah. I think so too."

Mom: "I haven't cheered in years! Let's do it."

All: "All for one and one for all."

As they leave the room to have a snack, Dad asks how the meeting was.

Leslie: "Okay."

Kelly: "Okay"

Mom: "I'm relieved. I didn't realize I had all that bottled up inside me!"

What did you notice about the script you just read? Did you get ideas on how to address each topic for discussion? Hopefully you noticed the following:

- **Clarify the topic – use active listening, ask questions.**
- **Asking for family member's feelings about the topic.**
- **Name and acknowledge those feelings. Sometimes this is all that is needed on a topic.**
- **Talking about the values you hold in relation to the agenda item, if appropriate.**

- **Brainstorming, if appropriate (don't comment or censor ideas so they keep flowing). Sometimes brainstorming is more appropriate in the next meeting, after the feelings are identified and acknowledged and have had a chance to be settle down.**
- **When the time for decision has come, deciding on action through a process that fits your family (consensus or modified democracy, or choose between acceptable alternatives).**
- **Recording decisions so they are clear and can be referred to in the future. This is an important part of follow-through that parents can model for children.**
- **End with a positive topic.**
- **Asking how the meeting went for each participant (what each liked and wishes as to how the next meeting might be different).**
- **Briefly discussing next steps/next meeting.**
- **Follow the meeting with something enjoyable.**
-

Reflection: This sample meeting is likely more ideal than your Family Meetings may turn out to be. Don't be discouraged. **Family tradition and family communication take some time to**

develop. Just like anything else, communication in Family Meetings takes practice and has to adjust to changing needs and phases. Keep in mind that there is no structure that more positively meets the needs of an evolving family than Family Meetings.

"I was frustrated with doing all of the housework, or so it seemed to me. I brought this to a Family Meeting when our son was six and our daughter was a toddler. We made it more neutral and across-the-board by brainstorming a list of all the ways we spent time. Everyone had ideas. I made a picture chart of how we each spent our time. It had items on it suggested by our son such as 'tickle time' 'roughhouse,' 'treats' and 'cuddle time,' 'playtime with family members." For the baby, we listed 'diaper time,' 'burp time,' and 'crying time' among other things. For me, it was having private time when I went to the bathroom! And then we talked about how each person would get household tasks done. By brainstorming the tasks involved in family home life, children and adults alike are more likely to invest in doing the work and to see that it is unfair for one or two members to do all of it. Each person in our family took on something he or she could do. Later, we revisited chores again from time to time. Our children began doing their own laundry early on!"

Parents reported the following surprises after six months of holding Family Meetings!

"A breakthrough came while working with my child on math, I really connected with her."

"This was the first time I did an activity in which my child gave to others: a visit to donate to the animal shelter."

"On a busy weekend, handling of more than usual homework, my middle school child came up with her own plan!"

"My nine year old boy will now do things the first time a parent asks!"

"I took my children on the train to a puppet show. It was nice to spend my limited time so well with my children."

CHAPTER SEVEN:
Family Meetings Over Time: Overcoming Obstacles with Solutions

As with any family routine, Family Meetings are hard to fit into daily life. Things happen. Adults overwork, kids get sick, elderly parents need attention and suddenly we realize it's been months since we had a Family Meeting! Don't give up. Life is full of starting over, coming around full circle, cycles—you know what I mean. Taking up Family Meetings again is so important. Family Meetings can give a center to your family life, one that pays off big-time!

When you've had several meetings, the rhythm can get interrupted; many parents give up at this point. Yet we know that the benefits of Family Meetings come from having them over a sustained period of time. You wanted to create a wonderful family life, right? Then you've got to keep at it by starting again.

Workshop participants have shared their ideas about overcoming obstacles and restarting Family

Meetings after "life interrupted." As you've read in this book, some workshop participants are having Family Meetings many years later! Here are the top obstacles workshop participants identified to their Family Meetings—and how to overcome them.

The obstacle of busyness has many "faces."

Busy Obstacle 1: It takes repeated effort to hold Family Meetings; we're too tired to sustain the effort.

Solutions:

- Discuss the next meeting before ending the current one.
- Agree to continue meetings until all the brainstormed topics are covered and resolved.
- Create success in the first few meetings by having well defined and bite-sized topics.

- Recognize that commitment grows over time.
- Remember and remind one another that Family Meetings are about connection and the spirit of the family.
- Discuss hopes, fears and dreams.
- The fun item keeps us going. Keep a list of successes from previous meetings. Talk about what are we are thankful for.

Busy Obstacle 2: It is hard to find a good time; we're all too busy with activities

Solutions:

- Find one time that's open, put it on the calendar for the whole year; give Family Meetings importance by scheduling them.
- Agree to do a finite number of meetings for a limited time and then revisit whether to continue.

- Remember that having meetings now saves time later on –drug-free kids, easy teens etc.
- It takes time to create the family atmosphere you want.

Busy Obstacle 3: We stopped Family Meetings after a while. It's hard to get back to it.

Solutions:

- Schedule a general meeting to evaluate the meetings you have had and to review the "state of the family."
- Break down this obstacle into smaller chunks.
- Remember and remind family members that Family Meetings are about. connection and the spirit of the family
- How do you deal with backsliding with any other habits or routines? Use the same methods.

The Effort it takes to hold Family Meetings over time also has several aspects.

Effort Obstacle 1: One parent is always the initiator and meeting leader; he or she becomes resentful, burns out or gives up.

Solutions:

- Have kids run the meetings.
- Have the meeting in the car on the way to a fun family outing.
- Another family member acknowledges and backs up the one who is doing so much.
- Participate with good will.

"One of my family's best Family Meetings was in a restaurant on the way to a weekend destination. There was a lot of lively discussion and laughter. We got some interested looks from the people at nearby tables!"

Effort Obstacle 2: Lack of organization or planning on the part of parents

Solutions:

- Put a child in charge of getting meetings on the calendar and reminding.
- After one or two meetings, see how often they are needed. Have a minimum, such as quarterly.
- Protect Family Meeting time by writing them on the calendar; you can do this during the meeting.
- Arrange meetings in advance and let everyone know they need to plan around them.
- Remember, success builds on success.

"We were able to see our daughter and ourselves as individuals; this is so crucial when dual career family life results in daily chaos." E.S.

Developing the skills for Family Meetings can be daunting to some.

Skill Obstacle 1: One parent (or both) doesn't like the feeling of being a beginner. Parent(s) don't know what to say or do.

Solutions:

- Start with short meetings and short, easy topics with something achievable and build from there.
- Use the information in this book, online, in parenting books or videos to build skills.
- Feel free to table an item; it's okay to say, "I need to think about it" and to bring the item back to the next meeting.
- Put on a timer to do something silly or dance.
- Remember, you're not the only one who is new at this! You're the adult

so remember to have patience with learning—your kids do!

Skill Obstacle 2: Obstacle: We can't think of agenda items

Solutions:

- Talk about agenda items for next time in the current meeting.
- Have pre-printed agenda forms that are posted during the month, seed them with "one fun item."
- Use the format of "How are things going with____" and let others fill in the blank.

Skill Obstacle 3: Backsliding- Family Meetings were going well but suddenly family members are acting like they don't even know what a Family Meeting is. Communication goes back to the way it was before, or worse, or one person begins to test the patience of the other family members.

Solutions:

- This happens from time to time so don't panic. The next meeting may be back to normal.
- It's a good time to look at what was done when things were going well in meetings.

Sometimes one or more people are the problem with continuing meetings.

People Obstacle 1: One family member, usually a child, complains bitterly or repeatedly about having to have Family Meetings.

Solutions:

- Involve children so that you are not doing the Family Meeting *to* them. This could be an agenda item itself-how to involve them.
- Make it fun and easy “”Pen, notebook and candle—I can do that.”

- Find out what this person cares about and have that as a topic.

People Obstacle 2: One person's problem is always the focus.

Solution:

- Have this person be the leader of the meeting with the job of making sure the time is shared and the agenda is covered.
- Have this person be the scribe so that he or she has a role that doesn't involve talking.

People Obstacle 3: One or more parents feel that it's "my way or the highway" and is unwilling to give up parental authority on any issue.

Solution:

- Return to the preparation part of this book and the exercises in it. Parents, by themselves, need to discuss how these messages, beliefs, and hopes are being realized and whether you can both participate in good faith in a Family Meeting.

Family Meetings can lose vitality from time to time.

Obstacle: The Family Meetings get boring, stale or in a rut.

Solutions:

- Thank each person for coming and participating.
- Ask how the meeting went.
- Sing something.
- Have a family "ritual" to end the meeting such as a special hand motion, handshake or group hug.
- Review the times you did the one fun item you brainstormed in a Family Meeting and then plan another.
- Start the Family Meeting by asking everyone ahead of time to bring a joke

CHAPTER EIGHT:
Communication Techniques to Help in Your Family Meetings and Your Daily Life

Introduction to Building Communication Skills

For many years, I have collected ideas on how to improve communication. Perhaps you have too. The collection below offers ideas and reminders that make common sense but are easily forgotten. We all need reminders and practice. **The way we say things matters** as much as what we say. Our tone of voice, body language and attitude say more than do our words. Family meetings provide a place to learn and practice communication—for both children and parents. Read on…

How do Family Meetings improve communication?

Let's compare improving the way we communicate with a worker's progress in a construction trade-- apprentice level, journeyman level and master level. After all, we are building our family with Family Meetings.

1. Parents as apprentice communicators

The apprentice communicator begins by learning to look inward to try to identify beliefs, thoughts, assumptions, emotions and values. Take time to think about the basis for your conclusions; only then will you have a starting point for real communication to another.

Remember that we all hear and see things through the lens of our experience. Apprentices often react. They react to things they heard or didn't hear when they were growing up—the very reason we spent time on this subject in the preparation section of this handbook.

The goal for apprentice communicators is to go beyond the reflexive process, the doctor's little hammer hitting your knee and making it jump. Does your child say something and before you can even think, you react—with anger, with righteousness, with a mean tone of voice? Okay,

this is where we start. But over time, and with practice, the self-examination process allows a response, rather than a reaction.
With practice, the response becomes almost as automatic as the reaction once was. Wait ten seconds and then ask yourself what you are assuming. Then ask the other person whether your assumptions are correct. Ask for clarification to see if what you are reacting to is what you first thought. Take another ten seconds to reconsider the validity of your beliefs, thoughts and values in light of what was said. Look inside before responding. Yes, it seems slow and artificial at first but, like any new skill, it will become faster and more automatic with practice. You are learning to use a delicate tool instead of a hammer. Your kids will appreciate it!

2. Guiding our children through their apprenticeship Often at the same time as we parents are learning to move through our apprenticeship, we are also faced with the question, "How do we help children, who are already authentic in their responses, learn the rest of the process-- that of identifying their feelings and the basis for their feelings, and then testing their assumptions, thoughts and beliefs?"

One way is to model the process. Ask about the child's feelings first and then validate and acknowledge their feelings. It sounds so simple! Yet it is hard to do, even in the intentional process of a Family Meeting. We often just don't want our children to have negative experiences, so we parents do any number of invalidating things to "make sure" they don't.

- We deny the truth of the child having his or her feeling ("You don't really feel so bad, do you?").
- Or we minimize the extent of it ("It's not that bad, it's only a scratch"). Or we act on the mistaken belief that the child will be

tougher or learn a lesson if we tell them to "Get over it. Get used to it."

- Or we argue. We tell children (and one another) that they should feel something else or have a different intensity in their feelings. "You're not really mad, you're sad.")
- Or we go right to our own negative behavior and threaten them with consequences. (Child, "I hate my brother." Parent, "Don't even think about hitting him or you'll be in big trouble.")
- And then sometimes we just try to fix it. ("I'll go right over and talk to Jimmy's mother about this.")

Much has been written on the subject of these responses and the consequences they have for the relationship between parent and child. See the "Further Reading" section of this book; <u>How to Talk so Children will Listen; How to Listen so Children Will Talk</u> or <u>Do I Have to Give Up Being</u>

Me to be Loved By My Children" by Drs. Jordan and Margaret Paul.

3. What is a "journeyman" parental response rather than an apprentice?

a. Ask, don't tell

Instead of challenging what your child tells you, ask your child more about what he or she is feeling. If there is a response, validate it. It shows you are listening and paying attention; it shows your concern and respect. "Yes, you're angry. It's okay to be angry in that kind of situation." Don't problem-solve yet!

Ask clarifying questions such as

- "How was that situation for you?" What was going on for you at that point?"
- And now how do you feel about it?

And then acknowledge and validate those statements.

Tip: ***The Quakers have a process for members of their congregations which they call "discernment." Elders gather to hear the person present his or her dilemma. The only role of the elders is to ask questions to help the person discern their truth and direction. This process can be used in a simplified way in Family Meetings. When we truly listen and ask deeper, clarifying, open questions we often see the spiritual side of the other. We certainly find out where that person is coming from in their feelings, thoughts and intentions.***

- Ask what is wanted, sympathy or solutions.

Often, listening is all a person wants. In our family, we developed a tradition of asking, in our meetings (and in daily life), "Do you want sympathy or solutions now?" Often it was sympathy. By that, our family meant acknowledging the feeling and giving approval to it. "Yes, I understand why you would feel that way."

b. How to Communicate Respect (and not lecture your children)

Conveying respect for the other person (or people) in the conversation is essential to good relationships. Respect is a vital element in every Family Meeting. Respect is not the easy road. It's easier to interrupt, to tease, to exaggerate or to minimize what you hear when you respond. It's easier to be glib than authentic. We are exposed to staccato banter on the media every day. It is harder to think about our own values or ideals and then to convey them without sounding or feeling self-righteous or forced.

Yet we know that parents' lectures usually fall on deaf ears. Lectures raise natural resistance, making it harder to listen. It is hard to understand what the person is saying when we're preparing our next remark instead. Let's talk about how to communicate with respect and to improve our listening and our speaking over time. Keep in mind that each family member will improve but that **parents must set the model,** even when it would be easier to fall back on old patterns of how you have been speaking to your child.

We show respect in communication **to another** when we:

- speak in a neutral tone of voice
- state the problem rather than our conclusion or the solution
- express our own assumptions along with the facts that led to our own assumptions
- check for understanding of your own points of view and then stop talking (refrain from convincing)
- give the reason or reasons why we think the way we do
- speak our own truth and don't portray it as "The Truth"
- work toward a common understanding or a common goal
- refrain from personal comments
- take only our fair share of the "air time"
- use specific examples, even when we praise

We show respect in communication **from another** when we:

- listen with focused attention

- refrain from thinking about our reaction or response to what is being said
- refrain from interrupting
- ask for their facts, assumptions, feelings and beliefs
- when we check for understanding of what we have heard and ask if it's accurate
- ask questions for clarification
- when we acknowledge the other person's feelings as okay no matter what
- when we nod to show our interest
- when we remember the other person's view and bring it up respectfully and appropriately later on

We parents get frustrated at times. What can we do about it? Parents voice something like this, **"When I talk to my children, we often end up with anger, frustration, sullenness, nagging or yelling. I want us to do better on a day to day basis but also wonder how Family Meetings can be different than our usual conversations?"**

How would it be if, instead of becoming annoyed and yelling at children, we were able to stay calm and say to the child: "**Can you say that in your other voice**?" or "**You have two minutes to complain.**" How would it be if we told our child **we need a couple of deep breaths to calm** ourselves down? Doing so means you've attained the journeyman level!

More Communication ideas for the Journeyman level

Family Life can spiral either up or down. Good communication and catching problems at the start favor spiraling to a better level with more closeness.

Here is a brainstorm of communication techniques that build closeness among family members:

- Guess family member's feelings and ask for a response with thumbs up or down to confirm.
- Talk about what pattern or specific example you see, rather than general comments about the situation.
- Pillow talk- it has the advantage of no eye contact and provides snuggling time.

- Ritual- games and special food after meeting.
- Saying, "These are my feelings. I don't want you to take them on. You don't have to fix things just like I can't fix things when you're feeling sad/mad. I am capable. Thank you for caring so much that you wanted to take this on."
- Kids have their own relationship with other relatives. Separate this from your own feelings/history with these relatives.
- In the book, Growing Up Again, the author provides a good visual about balance. It is a road. The ditches on the two sides are "abuse" and "neglect." The two lanes are "supportive care" such as "Let me know when you need help with ___" and "Assertive care" such as "It's time to…."
- Begin a special family document that kids can write in, use a 3 ring notebook.
- Encourage kids to ask you questions- what was it like when you were my age?
- Use "and" instead of "but" for feedback. Example: "I like the way

you did 'x' <u>and</u> I think you'll do better with 'y' next time...."

- Parents can ask children, "What could you have done differently? How would you handle this situation differently?"
- Use sympathy without giving in.
- How can we change messages or habits we got growing up?

The steps are 1) awareness 2) address our own childhood issues 3) ask ourselves, "What do I think of the parenting I got now that I am a parent?" and 4) make my own decisions, my own conscious choices

- Wait until you're calm to respond. Say that you are taking your own "time-out" until you are ready.

4. <u>Parents' Master Level Communication</u>

As a parent, one of our most important jobs is to help our children identify their feelings in order to develop their "emotional intelligence." Much has been written about Emotional Intelligence, a concept developed by Daniel Goleman (see section on Further Reading).

Offer help in identifying feelings. The main categories of feeling are:

1. happy
2. sad
3. mad
4. hurt or
5. scared

There are many subtle variations on these feelings which are worth understanding. It is not the same to feel terrified as it is to feel a bit afraid, or irate vs. annoyed. These distinctions help all of us gain perspective and gauge our response better to any given situation, whether we are adults or children.

What happens when children or adults don't know what they are feeling? Many people of all ages seem to have great difficulty with the skill of identifying their own feelings. The way to build the skill is to ask what the person is feeling, then, if there is no answer,

- offer possibilities to choose from. For example, "Are you feeling mad or sad or both about this?"
- Or you can suggest, "Someone in this situation might be feeling sad or mad or thinking [name the possible thought]. I was wondering if this could be what you are feeling."
- And a third method is to ask where in the person's body they feel something when they talk about the situation. Often a parent will then be able to identify the feeling that this part of the body would mean if you felt it there yourself. For example, "My stomach is tight" might indicate fear or "in my fist" might indicate anger.
- Or you may see a fleeting look on a family member's face and you will recognize the feeling immediately.

Have faith that, with practice, the skill of identifying emotions in oneself and in others will improve. Remember, perceiving the emotion behind what someone says creates more empathy and more understanding.

Once we've identified a feeling, what's next?

Talk about feelings before solutions. We need to accept all feelings but not all behavior. It's okay to feel angry but it's not okay to hit. Help your child express the feeling and acknowledge that it is okay to have the feeling even if it is intense. Ask questions rather than offer solutions. Ask if the child is ready to talk about ways to handle his or her emotions. Only help with problem-solving when the feelings are in perspective, maybe at a later time. **Offer support and love first and make sure you identify the problem as separate from the person having the problem.**

Build your master skills by asking open ended questions.

Another area in developing communication skills is to learn the open ended questions that help another clarify their own feelings and thoughts. For such simple questions, they are surprisingly hard to remember and even harder to remember at the time they are needed. Here are sample open-ended questions:

- "How are you doing about ___?
- "What's your thinking about ___?"
- "What feeling are you experiencing?
- " And how is that for you?"
- "Could you say more about it?"
- "What led you to that conclusion?"
- "I value your opinion and would like to know what it is on this situation."
- "What other times have you felt or experienced something like this?"
- "If it were your best friend this happened to, what would you advise or do?"
- "Let's see if I'm following you…"

When something bad has happened, perhaps a bad grade, sympathize first. "Oh no, I imagine you must be embarrassed about that one bad grade." Notice, this doesn't lead to a power struggle! Sympathy conveys that it's okay to make mistakes and to make decisions. Remember to check your assumptions. For example, ask if embarrassment is the feeling your child is experiencing and if it isn't, invite the child to tell you what they are feeling, anger perhaps. Listen carefully for information on feelings. Accept all feelings; refrain from judging another's feelings.

What about those "I" statements? A lot has been written about using "I" statements. I prefer to think of this concept as speaking one's own truth from one's own perspective. This is a learned skill and it is not easy. It is easier, but not respectful, to order others to do or be a certain way. It is also easy to couch a "you should" in an "I" statement. For example, "I want you to never do X again?" or "I think you're being a pill."

Sample master level phrases when speaking genuinely to others:

- "From my perspective…
- "Here's my thinking on …"
- "I'm feeling X and I just wanted you to know."
- "Another way to look at this is…"
- "I want to tell about this because…"

Notice the positive things and acknowledge them first. Our natural tendency is to notice the five percent that is "wrong" or "bad" and not the ninety-five percent that is "right" or "good." We may be wired to notice the bad for survival as a hunter/gatherer species. Nowadays, it makes more sense to notice, acknowledge and appreciate when even small things are going well or when your child has been behaving well. Talk about it!

How do Family Meetings help develop mastery level communicators?

The overall purpose of a family meeting is to build family relationships. Building good relationships is more important than anything, **more important than solving problems, making plans or making decisions. Always keep the goal in mind.** It takes time, practice, falling short and trying again. However, when the hard things in life come along, Family Meetings prove their worth.

When a family member is having a hard time, give him or her a "CARESS."

Everyone goes through hard times in life at some point. When one of your family members has his or her turn, here is a technique that may help in a pinch.

> Show your caring concern by saying five statements including each of the following words, applied to the person's situation and end with a loving touch. You will be amazed at the closeness created by this technique.

- Compassion

- Acceptance
- Respect
- Encouragement
- Support
- Stroking

Example: "I feel for you in having to deal with a bully at school. I imagine it makes you feel just awful inside. I think you are fine just the way you are. I respect you for dealing with the situation the best you could. I encourage you that this situation can get better and there will come a time when you won't have to deal with a bully. I support you and am here if you want or need help in feeling safe at school." (Pat hand or hug.)

Try this technique. See if it helps.

Conclusion

Family Meetings Make Families Strong

When TROUBLE comes, the tradition of having Family Meetings is a proven *lifesaver*

Ms. A attended my first workshop without her spouse. She participated and seemed interested but towards the end, she asked for help with a situation involving one of her children, eight years old, who had what she thought was extreme taste in clothes and insistence on wearing them. The mother rejected all that was said on the subject in the workshop and I thought she left with the intention of dismissing the idea of holding Family Meetings in her family. <u>Five years later, she contacted me</u> .. We went for a long walk in the park together. After we had chatted for a while she said, "By the way, I'm so glad you taught the Family Meeting Workshop. We started having Family Meetings and when many awful things happened in our family in a short period of time, they were invaluable in getting us through." The bad things were indeed very bad—the death of five relatives from cancer, including some in their 40's and the diagnosis of both obsessive/compulsive disorder and ADD in

the now teenage son. Hard things to deal with in any family. Family Meetings helped them get through.

A college student found Family Meetings to be invaluable when her older sister was diagnosed with cancer. It was so good to have a forum to talk about it with the whole family right away. This family knew what to do and how to do it. They came together, asked about one another's feelings, and discussed how to get through the coming year of treatment with support for all.

The Family Meeting Handbook is a reference and resource for you and your family to use now and as time goes on. Family Meetings are a way to build the safe space we all hope our home provides. Family Meetings can help create and maintain balance in your family life. Family Meetings provide a simple structure and a regular time to convey priorities and to bring family members into closer relationship that lasts a lifetime. An hour every month or so can make a difference. It has made a difference in my family and I hope that it will in yours.

Further Reading:

Clark, Jean Illsley and Connie Dawson. Growing Up Again. Hazelden. 1989 and 1998.

Cline, Foster and Jim Fay. Parenting with Love and Logic. Nav Press 1990, 2006.

Faber, Adele and Elaine Mazlish. How to Talk So Kids Will Listen and Listen So Kids Will Talk. 30th Anniversary ed, Scribner 2012.

Faber, Adele and Elaine Mazlish. How to be the Parent You Always Wanted to Be. Scribner, 1992, 2013.

Feiler, Bruce. The Secrets of Happy Families. William Morrow, Harper Collins, 2013.

Goleman, Daniel. Emotional Intelligence: Why It Can Matter More Than IQ. Bantam Books 1997.

Gordon, Thomas. Parent Effectiveness Training. Three Rivers Press, 1970,1975, 2000.

Paul, Jordan, and Margaret Paul. Do I Have to Give Up Being Me in Order to be Loved by You. Hazelden, 1983, 2002

Peterson, Rick. "Families First: Keys to Successful Family Functioning Communication." Assistant Professor, Department of Human Development,

Virginia Tech and Stephen Green, Department of Human Development, In Public Extension Pub 350-092,Virginia Tech, 2009.

Phelan, Thomas. 1-2-3 Magic: Effective Discipline for Children 2-12. PMi Inc, 5th ed. 2014.

Siegel & Hartzall. Parenting From the Inside Out. Tarcher Penguin, 2003, 2014.

Family's values and policies exert a strong positive influence on children. Children more likely to be problem solvers and attain independence.

The family is a stronger, more cohesive unit

Involve children in family matters right from the beginning

More consistent follow through on rules for children

Meaningful discussions held more often

All family members develop better communication skills

Adults examine and align their own values with their actions

Periodic updates keep balance on many fronts, allow for smooth transitions as children grow

Made in the USA
San Bernardino, CA
20 August 2016